A Bridge Worth Saving

A Bridge Worth Saving

A Community Guide to Historic Bridge Preservation

Mike Mort

East Lansing • Michigan State University Press

♾ The paper used in this publication meets the minimum requirements of ANSI/NISO Z39.48-1992 (R 1997) (Permanence of Paper).

 Michigan State University Press
East Lansing, Michigan 48823-5245

Printed and bound in the United States of America.

14 13 12 11 10 09 08   1 2 3 4 5 6 7 8 9 10

ISBN: 978-0-87013-828-7

LIBRARY OF CONGRESS CATALOGING-IN-PUBLICATION DATA
Mort, Mike, 1952-
A bridge worth saving : a community guide to historic bridge preservation / by Mike Mort.
p. cm.
Includes bibliographical references and index.
ISBN 978-0-87013-828-7 (pbk. : alk. paper)
1. Historic bridges—Conservation and restoration—United States. I. Title.
TG23.M67 2008
624.2028'8—dc22
2008008746

Cover design by Heather Truelove Aiston
Book design by Charlie Sharp, Sharp Des!gns, Lansing, MI
Cover photo is of the old Charlotte Highway Bridge currently residing at the Calhoun County Historic Bridge Park near Battle Creek, Michigan.

green press initiative Michigan State University Press is a member of the Green Press Initiative and is committed to developing and encouraging ecologically responsible publishing practices. For more information about the Green Press Initiative and the use of recycled paper in book publishing, please visit *www.greenpressinitiative.org*.

Visit Michigan State University Press on the World Wide Web at *www.msupress.msu.edu*

Contents

Acknowledgments

I f there were ever justification for using the "editorial we" in a manuscript, this just might be the document. It is the product of seven most appropriate people: a professor of engineering who analyzes and designs bridge parts for historic restoration projects, a mathematician whose pastime is photographing old bridges, a woman with a love for research and historical detail, a retired steel fabricator with many successful bridge restoration projects under his belt, a state employee who specializes in transportation archeology, a state historic preservation official who regularly reviews applications for historic bridge sites, and a county road commission director who contends with bridge dilemmas every day. The actual words have come from a cinematographer who eagerly accepted the assignment because he had just completed a film about Michigan's historic highway bridges and had grown quite fond of them.

It is valuable to know these biographical traits of the writing team to dispel any notion that *A Bridge Worth Saving* is the product of one sheltered engineer or an overly idealistic historian. On the contrary, these words have been sifted through the experiences and insights of people who have actually gone through the process of saving an old bridge. Some have literally

The bridge gang. Left to right: Bob Christensen, Mike Mort, Frank Hatfield, Nan Jackson, Dennis Randolph, Vern Mesler, Margaret Barondess, Elaine Davis.

taken bridges apart and put them back together again. You can trust their advice.

Because almost every idea in this story has come from someone other than the writer, repeated references to original sources would be unbearably distracting. Keep in mind, therefore, that when reference is omitted, the major contributors listed below should be thanked. This is indeed their book. Consider the writer a musician playing a piece composed by someone else. The manuscript may reflect a unique performance technique or interpretation, but make no mistake about it, *A Bridge Worth Saving* is their music.

Major Contributors

- Margaret Barondess, state transportation historian
- Bob Christensen, state historic preservation official
- Elaine Davis, historian
- Frank Hatfield, professor of engineering
- Nan Jackson, professor of mathematics
- Vernon Mesler, steel fabricator
- Dennis Randolph, county road commission director

Special Contributors

- Julie Avery, museum curator
- Lloyd Baldwin, historian
- Sigrid Bergland, historian
- Betty Burton, English teacher
- Wayne Conklin, steelworker
- Rob Denniston, steelworker
- Kim Foghino, librarian
- Al Halbeisen, engineer-consultant
- Sarah Kalasky, artist
- Walt Kaechely, newspaper reporter
- Michael Koon, transportation official
- Bob Magness, U.S. Marine Corps, ret.
- Bonnie Mort, third-grade teacher
- Mary Murphy, librarian
- Frank Nelson, transportation official
- John Pahl, town historian
- Kevin Pruski, transportation official
- Nels Raynor, construction manager
- Karen Visser, college marketing director
- Charles Walker, transportation official
- Karla Weidner, librarian
- Sandra Wheat, community volunteer

I also must acknowledge my wife, Bonnie. She has stood faithfully by my side through good sentences and bad and has not failed to point out lovingly when the latter needed more work. She also contributes much to the happiness in my life, which I hope inspires every phrase of this text.

Preface

O ver the St. Joseph River in southwest Michigan reaches a 130-foot Pratt through truss. On one side of the bridge stands an old house built by a French fur trader and an outbuilding once used as an Indian trading post. On its other side lies the small town of Mendon. More than 100 years ago, children crossed this bridge each day on their way to a one-room school a quarter-mile down an unpaved county road. Throughout its life, horse-drawn wagons coated this bridge with dust as they brought grain into town to the elevator visible from its span. Automobiles traversed it with caution until it was closed to vehicular traffic in 1982. Fabricated by craftsmen and assembled by local labor, it is today as much a community work of art as any stone monument that one might find in a town square.

This bridge, called the Marantette Bridge for the family whose homestead road once connected it to town, is in danger of being lost forever. Its iron and steel members are rust-pitted and weakening. Boards that once fit its deck tightly are now loose and moss-covered. Some are missing altogether, forcing those who would try to cross it to do so as one would walk the ties of a railroad trestle. Its abutments are also in disrepair. What had become a prime fishing platform for bluegill is now a liability problem with a potentially high price tag. Some townsfolk say, "Just tear it down and be done with it." Most, though, hold the notion that its profile is somehow significant to their small town. A committee has formed to see if something can be done.

This book is about the Marantette Bridge, and the Big Hill Road Bridge just up the road, and the 20 Mile Road Bridge in a neighboring county, and numerous other metal-truss bridges that are in decline. It is about paint, rust, metal fatigue, eyebars, and rivets. It is also about volunteers, fund-raising, liability, and, yes, even about the meaning of life. For hidden in anyone's proclivity to preserve old things lie philosophical assumptions about life itself. That is why it is important to read this book as a student, an activist, and a sage.

Unlike some imperatives that only lead one to an idealistic starting point without further advice, this book will show you, in a step-by-step way, *how* to save an old metal-truss bridge. Open it as a tool kit. Unfold it as a map. Refer to it as an operations manual. *A Bridge Worth Saving* is a call to action.

The characters and case studies in *A Bridge Worth Saving* have all come from Michigan. This should not make its message inappropriately provincial. Quite the contrary, this work presents a state-tested story from start to finish. If you wish to save a bridge in your community, you will need to cooperate with local and state governmental agencies. You will also need to communicate with your state department of transportation, your state historic preservation office, and a variety of other regulatory and support agencies in between. Knowing how one state coordinates this entire process will give you a better understanding of how your state works. Although there are nuances of process among the Michigan Department of Transportation (MDOT), the Missouri Department of Transportation (MODOT), and the Minnesota Department of Transportation (MNDOT), the task will, for all practical purposes, be the same.

Although the advice in this book is applicable to all metal-truss bridges, including such large and modern ones as the Blue Water Bridge at Port Huron or the International Bridge at Sault Ste. Marie, it focuses primarily on the small to medium-size historic metal-truss bridge, those built between the 1880s and the 1920s.

For whom, then, is this book being written? It is for the road superintendent who suspects an old bridge possibly might be saved but has no success stories to bolster his point of view or the local contractor who is well experienced at welding but has no formal training in the art of riveting. It is also for the small group of citizens who simply cannot bear the thought of losing their old bridge which has served their community for as long as they can remember. *A Bridge Worth Saving* is for the pessimist who is sure it can't be done and the optimist who only needs to know how. If you would like to save an old metal-truss bridge in your community, this book is for you.

A spring storm has just passed over the Marantette Bridge. Its iron members have been darkened by the rain. Water droplets can be seen reflecting light in spider webs in the most artworthy of places. It is an opportune time to see this bridge for more than its function implies. Much of preservation is a practical endeavor of cleaning up, fixing up, and replacing old, worn-out parts. However, it is always more than that. If you accept the challenge of caring for something others are willing to discard, you will need to be driven by love and respect for the three-dimensional elements of your past. The committee to save the Marantette Bridge is beginning to understand this. Preservation, in some strange but wonderful way, is about the meaning of life. These old iron relics do hold clues to our collective upbringing. From the water that flows beneath them, we can see reflections of our public soul, and the Marantette Bridge that faithfully served its community for more than 100 years, like many others, is a bridge worth saving.

Introduction

The village of Eagle River in the Upper Peninsula of Michigan is so historically noteworthy that much of the town has been placed on the National Register of Historic Places. When its small, 95-year-old bridge, a deck truss, was no longer able to accommodate increasing traffic loads, something had to be done, and demolition was not an option. Federal legislation mandated that Eagle River's historic status as a copper-mining town and a major port in the nineteenth century be protected. Working with both the state highway department and the federal highway administration, the small community of Eagle River was able to secure funds to build a new bridge parallel to its predecessor, allowing its historically protected bridge to continue to serve as a walkway over the gorge and waterfall it had traversed for almost a century.

The Sterling Road Bridge in rural Hillsdale County, Michigan, was also obsolete. Because of its inherent design limitations, its rehabilitation as a highway bridge was not an option. Rerouting traffic around the bridge was also out of the question because of housing developments and protected wetlands. Complicating the matter further were budget limitations. There was enough money to tear it down but not enough to put it back up again

Michigan Department of Transportation

The Eagle River Bridge in Michigan's Upper Peninsula used to allow passage across the gorge carved out by the river before it was closed to car traffic. Copper mining helped build this early port community on Lake Superior.

at some other location. So, rather than send it to the scrap yard, it was disassembled, with instructions inscribed on each piece to make re-erection easy at a later time. It was then stored in a county road commission field for almost a year. In 2000, TEA-21 Enhancement Funding was secured to complete the project, and the bridge was brought back to life. It is now a pedestrian crossway on the Michigan–Ohio border near the town of Morenci, Michigan, 100 miles from its original stand.

It is formally listed on the National Register of Historic Places as the 57th Street Bridge over the Kalamazoo River, but most folks call it the Bingo Bridge, because the town folk of Allegan, Michigan, played bingo to help raise money for its restoration. Newspaper writers had a field day, and TV human-interest story producers rolled plenty of tape for the local evening news. The bingo crowd raised more than $10,000 to save their old bridge. The amount was small compared with the total budget needed for the project, but the public relations impact of this clever fund-raising scheme was immeasurable.

Local citizens dedicated time, money, and their voices to the cause of saving the 57th Street Bridge in Allegan County. The county road commission took their message seriously, and the bridge was preserved for pedestrian and bike use.

This rare Thacher truss, made of wrought iron instead of steel, survived because of community intervention. Chesaning citizens fought hard to get the bridge moved to their downtown. Their tenacity paid off, adding a gem of a bridge to the historic community.

Grand Rapids is bisected by the Grand River. Numerous bridges link the east and west sides of town. The 6th Street bridge links old industrial areas undergoing revitalization. City staff keep the bridge working, recently sprucing it up using federal funds.

Less than a dozen Thacher through trusses survive in the United States, and one of them can be found in the small community of Chesaning, Michigan. Funding to preserve this century-old wrought-iron rarity came from federal grants, the city budget, corporate sponsors, individual donors, and proceeds from car washes and bake sales. The total project took three years to complete, and now the Parshallburg Bridge—or the Ditch Road Bridge, as some call it—stands as a pedestrian walkway into a city park.

Surrounded by dense urban development, the 6th Street Bridge, a 538-foot, four-span through truss over the Grand River in downtown Grand Rapids, Michigan, is the largest surviving highway through truss in Michigan. To replace this bridge with a modern span would cost a fortune. By faithfully maintaining the bridge over a long period of time, a crisis has been avoided. Today, the 6th Street Bridge keeps up with the rigors of big-city traffic as well as any. Its value has not only endured but increased.

Saving an old bridge has been done before—many times, in fact. In big and small towns, by iron craftsmen and little old ladies, with money from federal grants and bake sales, creative ways have been found to save old iron and steel bridges. They have been moved to city parks, converted into pedestrian walkways, recommissioned for limited one-way traffic, dedicated as prime fishing stands, and stored in county sheds to be revived years later. It's a tough job, but anybody can do it.

CHAPTER 1

Getting to Know Your Bridge

The more you know about your bridge, from its camber to its creator, the better you will be able to care for it and generate interest in it. Knowing its history and understanding its construction, down to the chemical composition of its steel, will earn you a command of your bridge that will greatly expedite your preservation journey. (A review of classic metal-truss bridge types and designs is offered in appendix 1.) Start with the following questions. Their answers represent a minimum core of knowledge essential to your preservation project. You will need this information to complete historical designation applications, fill out grant forms, write advocacy letters, and, most important, muster community support.

- Who owns the bridge? Who is legally responsible for it?
- What is the legal description of the location of the bridge? Have environmental and/or historical reviews been completed? Are "surrounding land use" or "scenic" issues involved?
- How old is the bridge? Specifically, when was it built?
- Who designed the bridge? Who fabricated the bridge? Who erected it?
- What type of bridge is it? What type of truss design does it use? What kind of metal is it made of?

- Is there anything unique about its design or construction? Are there any decorative features?
- How often and when has the bridge been repaired? Have any modifications ever been made? Has it ever been moved or raised?
- Have any noteworthy people or events been associated with this bridge?
- Has the bridge endured any serious floods or accidents?
- Is the bridge listed on any state highway bridge inventory?
- Have there been previous attempts to restore or preserve the bridge? Who was involved in these efforts? What repair methods were used? What were the issues? What was the result? Why?
- What general condition is the bridge in now? Does the bridge present any immediate danger to its community?
- Is the bridge scheduled for replacement? Why? When? How long do you actually have to save it?
- Is the bridge on the federal "critical bridge" list? Has funding for replacement or repair already been secured?

Consider the following seven classic research steps as you begin your investigation. There is nothing magical about these steps, and they are not in any particular order. Accept them as guideposts to keep you on track as you explore the historical and contemporary status of your bridge. The style or sequence of your inquiry is not as critical as its ultimate thoroughness.

Step One

Go to your bridge. That's right—head down to the river, and spend some time thoroughly inspecting your bridge. How long and wide is it? What type of truss does it employ? How many panels does it have? Has it been assembled with pins, rivets, or bolts? Do parts of it appear to have been welded? Does the bridge have a nameplate? Are there any meaningful or identifiable markings on the metal? Structural features and industrial inscriptions can provide more information than you might initially think. The nameplate may offer the date of your bridge's construction and also the name of the company that built it. The nameplate also may list agencies or officials involved in the

An older bridge usually has a nameplate attached to the top of the bridge at each end. This plate's ornamentation is reminiscent of that found in Victorian architecture. The plate lists the year of construction and the names of the township commissioner, supervisor, and clerk who were responsible for the bridge's purchase, construction, and maintenance.

project. Take lots of photos, and begin a file of information for everything you find.

Step Two

Talk to the people who live, or have lived, around the bridge. Call up the town historian. Put out feelers at the corner café. A classified ad or letter to the editor may reap volumes. Ask the local radio or TV station to do a human-interest story about the bridge. Put a query in the local historical society newsletter and online. If you are unusually lucky, you may discover some old-timers who actually watched the bridge being constructed while they played kick-the-can in a nearby field. Putting the word out that there are some folks in town trying to save the old bridge also should give you a good clue about potential public support for a preservation project.

Step Three

Check on two possible already-existing sources of information: the Historic American Engineering Record, HAER (maintained by the National Park Service; more information about this and other organizations that can help your research is offered in appendix 2) and any formal bridge inventory that your state department of transportation may have already commissioned. The HAER can be accessed through the Internet. Follow up with your state historic preservation office for other reports.

Each state maintains an inventory of its bridges. Some publish descriptive reports of their historic ones. A phone call to your state department of transportation will confirm if such a list exists. Stick with it until you find the right person to talk to. Checking first with the HAER and also your department of transportation should save you from looking for information that has already been compiled.

These initial contacts with state authorities will offer more than informational insight. The people behind the phone numbers really do care about preservation issues. Although they may be cautious about your inquiries initially, and although the wheels of state bureaucracies may turn more slowly than you are used to at home, cheerful perseverance will pay off. The sooner you can establish relationships with your department of transportation and the state historic preservation office, the better.

Step Four

A trip to your local library is essential. Go directly to the reference librarian, and calmly announce that you're looking for information about the old bridge on the edge of town. Then watch his or her eyes gleam with intrigue. (Reference librarians live for such challenges.) You'll most likely be escorted to a small locked room called the history room. Don't be surprised if you are required to wear gloves, for this is where the oldest and most valuable documents are kept. Look for local and county histories. The indexes of these often will point directly to your bridge. Keep an eye out for old maps that may provide clues to when a bridge first appeared at the crossing. Old county atlases and plat books, which are sometimes housed in library history rooms, will indicate who owned the properties around the bridge. Look for bridges in the background records of local floods and fires. Wooden bridges did catch fire, and iron trusses often replaced them.

Repeat step four at your local and county historical society archives.

Step Five

With the construction date in hand, begin searching through tax records, newspaper files, or township meeting minutes. Without the construction date, you'll have to make an educated guess and start turning pages.

If you were not able to find the construction date on the nameplate of the bridge or through the HAER or any state department of transportation inventories, turn to your local road authority. A bridge in a big city should be well documented at city hall. Information about a rural bridge may be found at the county road commission office. In either location, keep looking for the right person who might be able to point you to a written history or an inspection report.

Before the formation of state transportation departments, most roads and bridges were owned by local authorities, such as villages or townships. This was often the case in Michigan until 1930, when oversight was transferred from townships to county road commissions by legislative fiat. Early bridge records therefore sometimes can be found in the dust-veneered, handwritten journals of small township halls. Some, though, have been moved to more secure repositories such as the county seat or a local or state archive. If the bridge was on a county or township line, its construction and upkeep costs and its records, most likely were shared by both parties. If the road served by the bridge is owned by the state, check with the state department of transportation. Ownership of a bridge is fluid, so don't be surprised if you find that it has changed several times over the course of its lifetime.

Funds for a new bridge would have been allocated by a city council or a village or township board and raised through a special tax. In many cases, a special election was held to approve raising this tax money. Such an assessment would be reflected in the general tax rolls and even sometimes noted in individual tax receipts. These first source documents can be quite helpful in understanding the economic climate of your bridge's first years. Tax records also can help narrow the search for a construction date. Seek them out.

Step Six

Today, almost always on microfilm and almost always accessible through your library, the newspaper is an indispensable source of information for the preservation sleuth. If you can locate issues coinciding with the construction and inauguration of your bridge, you may find notices for public hearings, advertisements to receive bids for construction, and editorials about the need for a new bridge, both pro and con. Who proposed the new bridge? How much did it cost? Why was it needed? Did the building of the bridge generate public controversy? Searching for the answers to these questions will require a considerable amount of patience and time, but answers can be found in the local newspaper. If not available at the library, bound historic newspapers sometimes can be found at your local newspaper office.

Step Seven

Any veteran investigator will tell you that some of the larger finds come from pursuing some of the smaller leads. This research step is a potpourri of small ideas that may reap big results.

Never underestimate the value of a picture. Visit your state and regional archives for any type of illustrative or photographic records. Your local historical society also should have an organized collection of historical photos. (Go through all of them, even if the topic is not relevant.) Old postcards featured public structures, including bridges. You might be surprised at how many closet postcard collectors are harbored in your town. You can also find postcards in antique shops.

Your state natural resources agency, such as the department of natural resources (DNR) or the department of environmental quality (DEQ), most likely requires environmental impact assessments (including historical reviews) for any work done in or near a river. Check with your state DNR

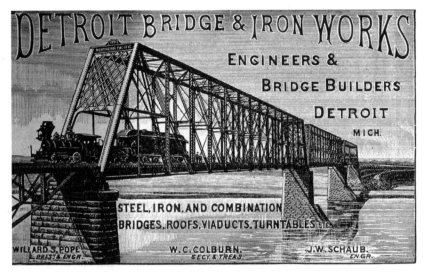

This advertising piece for the Detroit Bridge & Iron Works can be found in the *Directory of American Bridge-Building Companies*, a special publication by the Society for Industrial Archaeology that can provide information about bridge manufacturers.

about any such studies that may relate to your bridge. Local water agencies, such as drain commissions or irrigation districts, also must review plans that potentially affect local water flow. They, too, might be able to provide valuable information about your bridge.

Engineering college libraries are full of specialized publications applicable to your search, such as civil engineering journals, surveys, and trade catalogues. Bridge construction ads for large bridges throughout the United States were listed in the weekly publication *Current News Supplement,* which was bound in each issue of the *Engineering Record.* The U.S. Army Corps of Engineers also publishes flood-control reports, which might contain helpful information. You do not need to be an expert to benefit from these publications. Just ask the reference librarian for help.

If you have been successful in finding the name of the company that made the bridge, turn to the *Directory of American Bridge-Building Companies, 1840–1900* by Victor C. Darnell. This special publication of the Society for Industrial Archaeology may provide information about the manufacturer of your bridge.

If the waterway under your bridge is navigable, information about the bridge may be found through the Army Corps of Engineers or the Coast Guard.

In Review

- Carefully examine your bridge, and extract as much information as you can from its physical structure.
- Talk to local people in the area—the town historian, members of the historical society, and folks who live near the bridge.
- Check with the Historic American Engineering Record (HAER) of the National Park Service. Check also with your state historic preservation office and your state department of transportation about bridge inventories. Don't try to reinvent the historical research wheel.
- Head to your historical society and local library, and be amazed at the eagerness of the research librarian to help.
- Turn to your local transportation authority. Talk with the person responsible for the care and maintenance of bridges.
- Check out your local newspaper archives. Expect to spend a lot of time in front of the microfilm machine. Time permitting, enjoy the other old-town gossip you will undoubtedly find.
- Visit local, regional, and state archives. This includes your local historical society's stash of photographs, private postcard collections, area museums, and university collections.
- In all of your research efforts, always remember that polite persistence and a Sherlock Holmes–like curiosity will open many doors.

CHAPTER 2

Winning Community Support

The likelihood of success for any public endeavor is directly proportional to the number of people and organizations involved in the project. Political campaigns, church stewardship drives, school bond elections, and historic preservation projects live or perish on one axiom: Get people involved.

I have not found a better demonstration of this idea than what happened at the 2nd Street Bridge in Allegan, Michigan. The city of Allegan had gone through several unsuccessful preservation attempts before its bridge crisis. Years before, an old county courthouse and an ornate railroad depot had both succumbed to the wrecking ball, despite attempts by local residents to save them. Like many other Midwestern towns marking their centennial, the city of Allegan was struggling to find its historical voice. The old bridge on 2nd Street had forced its city leaders to ask again the question "How do we know what is really worth saving?" The Michigan Department of Transportation likewise added pressure to this clarification of values by scheduling to replace the 2nd Street Bridge during the summer of 1982. The clock for demolition was ticking again. This time though, preservation prevailed.

"The difference seemed to be that we got so many people involved," said Sandra Wheat, Allegan's mayor at the time of the project. "The city council

Aaron T. Brodeur

The 2nd Street Bridge over the Kalamazoo River in Allegan, Michigan, gained national attention in the early 1980s when the community chose to preserve rather than replace it. Allegan used local, state, and federal funds to repair the bridge, busting a few bureaucratic barriers favoring replacement over rehab.

passed a unanimous resolution of support. We got the township to kick in some money, too. The chamber solicited support from their members. Even school classes were coming down to the bridge to see what was going on."

"Schoolkids?" I asked Sandra and two of her colleagues as we all stood next to the bridge reminiscing about their accomplishment.

"One high school class used the bridge as a centerpiece for a historical research assignment. Another class circulated a petition to save the bridge and then came as a class to the city council to formally present the names supporting the project."

As they continued the story, I began to see the inevitable chain reaction. The kids went to their parents. The parents went to their neighbors. The neighbors went to their elected officials, and before you could say "the big beautiful bridge" three times backward, everyone in town knew something was up with the old iron bridge on 2nd Street. The town had not only been canvassed, it had been converted.

The effort to save the 2nd Street Bridge had faltered initially because it was favored by only a handful of people. The project eventually won a Presidential Award for Preservation and was honored at a ceremony in Washington, D.C., because a handful of people had recruited hundreds of other people to become actively involved in the project.

How does one rally such community support? I have four classic recommendations. Ignore any one of them at your peril.

Ask for Help

A politician once asked me, "What can I do for my constituents to get them to vote for me?" I replied, "Ask them to do something for you." "What?" he responded dubiously, as if to suggest I had not really understood his question. I repeated, "Ask them to do something for you." Then I explained, "If you simply tell your constituents what you wish to do for them, you might gain a vote or two. But if you ask your constituents to be involved in your campaign, to do something for you, their votes will multiply tenfold." This is a golden rule for political campaigns and historic preservation projects. If you tell community members what you intend to do for them, they will listen skeptically from a distance. If you ask community members to help get something done, they will more often rally to your side. Ask for help. Get people involved.

Give Volunteers Something Specific to Do

If I were to spend a few days in purgatory before any just reward, my punishment probably would resemble an unproductive meeting. Unproductive meetings, if not a venial sin, must be metaphorically evil at least. The best way to avoid them is to make sure everyone around the table has some specific assignment to fulfill. Give your volunteers something meaningful to do, something specific for which to be accountable. In other words, create job descriptions. Here are a few that may be applicable to your situation.

- Coordinate newspaper articles and letters to the editor.
- Provide public relations support to radio and TV.

- Explore state and federal funding.
- Begin work on grant writing.
- Gather a list of possible consultants and contractors to interview.
- Research the history of the bridge.
- Analyze the engineering principles of the bridge.
- Create an Internet Web page presence.
- Establish an e-mail support list, and set up an e-mail group.
- Publish a monthly newsletter.
- Create a database of supporters.
- Recruit sympathetic specialists, such as an attorney, architect, or engineer.
- Organize local fund-raising.
- Contact other folks involved in successful preservation projects.
- Serve as a liaison to the state DOT and historic preservation office.
- Take minutes of meetings.
- Recruit more supporters.
- Be a leader.

Note how the above tasks call for a broad range of talents and skills. You simply cannot do it all by yourself. This diverse and monumental amount of work is really a blessing in disguise, for it forces you to reach out to many people to achieve your goals. In the process of reaching out, a special type of environment is created in which it will be almost impossible not to succeed.

Create a Broad Tent

Of course, you are going to have the support of the historical folks. But if this is your only constituency, you have a problem. You also will need help from city administrators, elected officials, educational leaders, service club members, business owners, and, of course, your neighbors.

Many key community leaders may not have the time to be actively involved in another project, so recruit them as honorary members. Although they may not be able to lend a hand, they may be quite willing to lend their names. Ask for this symbolic but important support.

Eventually, you will want to publish a roster of all those in your community who support your goals. Such a membership role will indeed turn heads when you do your dog-and-pony show in front of the city council.

Be sure to include a representative from your regional or state department of transportation on your committee. These professional road and bridge people may not be able to attend all your meetings, but having them on the mailing list will keep them in the loop and on your side as your project proceeds. Eventually, you will need to bring a consultant or a professional project manager onboard. (We'll talk more about the roles of these two indispensable people in the next chapter.) Always remember, the likelihood of success for any public endeavor is proportional to the number and diversity of people involved.

Communicate Faithfully

Nothing impedes the cooperation of volunteers more than the failure to communicate with them on a regular basis. Communities likewise crave to know what's going on. Keep in touch with your supporters on a regular basis, through e-mail, postcards, phone-tree messaging, newsletters, and letters to the editor. Whatever the means, do it often, either electronically, in print, or the good old-fashioned way, by word of mouth.

Recognize and Respect the Various Perspectives and Agendas at the Table

Three people stood on the bank of a river looking at a bridge. One was an engineer, another was a planner, the third was a historian. They were all looking at the same bridge. Or were they? The engineer saw what looked to be a fairly sturdy Warren truss but worried about the viability of the weathered metal for today's traffic. The planner saw an old rusty bridge that was financially feasible to restore but wondered how such a proposed expenditure would survive at budget time when it came up against the water treatment facility the town so desperately needed. The historian saw an artifact of the American industrial revolution and wanted to save it at all costs. Each of these individuals was looking at the same bridge, but because of their unique points of view, they saw three different things.

As a member of the bridge restoration team, it is important for you to recognize the diversity of perspectives that will inevitably stand at the river-bank assessing your bridge. They are function, finance, and fidelity.

Function, finance, and fidelity to historical form are the three funda-mental points of view that will emerge in any bridge preservation project. At first, these unique perspectives may appear to be at odds with one another. A second look reveals a more sympathetic codependence.

Function

One need not certify a bridge to bear an invading army of tanks if it will be used only to escort a small group of walkers on a Sunday afternoon. How the bridge will ultimately be used should temper every decision during the restoration process. No one knows this better than the engineer. The histo-rian may say, "If the side railings were good enough for cars when the bridge was built, why aren't they good enough today?" The engineer knows that the side impact of a moving vehicle is calculated not only by the weight of the vehicle but also by its speed. Cars are not only heavier these days, they move faster, too. The planner may say, "What's all the fuss about weight and speed if the bridge is going to be put in a park and used only for foot traffic?" The engineer knows that a bridge packed full of children posing for their annual school picture is actually under more stress than it would be if it were loaded with cars. "Really?" asks the planner. "Yes," replies the engineer, "and that's if they're all standing still and not jumping up and down as schoolchildren have a tendency to do."

The engineer's point of view is fashioned by American Association of State Highway Transportation Officials (AASHTO) standards and state trans-portation codes. To the engineer, metal worthiness and structural integrity are paramount.

Finance

If money were not an object, every bridge would be kept in perfect order down to the weekly buffing of its cast-iron nameplate. Money is always an object, and anyone who suggests otherwise is either delusional or related to Bill Gates. Listen in on the following conversation as our three characters continue to look at the same bridge from the bank of the river.

"We must comply with the state three-coat painting standard," the engineer announces without hesitation. "How many coats of paint are really needed if the bridge will not be subjected to deicing salts in wintertime?" the planner replies skeptically, and adds, "Why not just sand-blast the bridge in place and get the local scout troop to paint it?" "Are you crazy?" replies the engineer. "Micro-silica dust can be lethal, and besides, what do kids know about painting a bridge?" While the engineer never cuts corners, the planner is always counting coins.

Fidelity

The historian is often unaware of engineering principles and emotionally unbound by budgetary constraints. He or she seeks to preserve as much of the original bridge as possible for history's sake. This idealistic point of view is usually the first to be sacrificed in any opinionated tug-of-war. The editors of this book unanimously recognize this. Sometimes, though, faithfulness to historic form is sacrificed unnecessarily for the sake of finance and function. (The last sentence is one of the most important sentences in this book. Please read it again.) The preservation of an old bridge is not just about meeting AASHTO standards or staying within budget. It is a community trust that requires a reasonable level of fidelity to historical detail. So, before you cavalierly throw away eyebars or indiscriminately replace rivets with bolts, listen to the historian. What if he or she could demonstrate to you that it is not only more historically accurate to re-rivet the bridge (from a preservationist's point of view), but it is just as safe (from an engineer's point of view), just as doable (from a steel fabricator's point of view), and sometimes just as inexpensive (from an planner's point of view)?

A Case in Point

Two bridges now stand side by side across the Silver Creek in Morenci, Michigan, a small Midwestern town on the Michigan–Ohio border. One is a 1935 steel I-beam bridge over which the town's people annually parade to celebrate its unique status as gateway into the state. It is formally called the Murray D. Van Wagoner Bridge after a former state highway commission

The Sterling Road Bridge moved to Morenci, next to state highway M-156. It carries a pedestrian and bicycle path across Silver Creek, allowing people to use the town's new sidewalk and bike path. The bridge also serves as a gateway feature at the Michigan–Ohio border.

director who later became governor of Michigan in 1941. The other bridge is the old Sterling Road Bridge, an 1893 Pratt through truss, which had been located over the St. Joseph River about forty miles northwest of Morenci. The story of these two bridges is significant, not because of unique preservation techniques but because of how the preservation team went about its work. It was a classic case of converging points of view.

The project team was assembled with the assignment of rehabilitating the 1935 Murray D. Van Wagoner Bridge for state highway traffic while remaining true to its historic integrity. The team included Tony Kratofil, the project development engineer from MDOT; Margaret Barondess, MDOT's resident historian and archeologist; Bob Christensen, consultant from Michigan's State Historic Preservation Office (SHPO); Brian Hintsala, design engineer-consultant from the firm of STS Consultants, Ltd.; and Vern Mesler, steel fabricator consultant for construction, who was brought in as the project evolved to include a metal-truss bridge.

Because all of these individuals enjoyed professional relationships with one another before this particular preservation project, it was easy to get the group together. But no sooner had the team assembled than typical preservation questions began to strain everyone's natural inclination to collaborate. Tony Kratofil (the project manager) knew that a new up-to-code railing had to be installed. Margaret Barondess (MDOT's resident historian) saw the old railing as an indispensable motif in the bridge's overall historical design. Simply to replace it with a stronger railing, in her opinion, would defy restoration logic. What could be done to bring these points of views together? Bob Christensen (SHPO's representative) suggested, "Let's use two railings, a modern one on the inside of the bridge's roadway to meet current code and the old one on the outside to maintain the bridge's historic profile." Ah, a consensus had emerged.

No sooner had the railing problem been resolved than Brian Hintsala (the design engineer) noticed, "With the extra railing, we'll no longer have room for a pedestrian walkway." Widening the bridge would have been too expensive (from Tony Kratofil's point of view), too architecturally precarious (from Bob Christensen's point of view), and simply out of the question (from Margaret Barondess point of view).

The solution of one problem had opened the door to another. With the project team members at the bridge where their meetings were normally held, Margaret Barondess suggested, "Why don't we find a homeless metal truss and put it alongside the steel-girder bridge and use the metal truss for pedestrian and bicycle traffic?" It was as if everyone's inner light bulb had been switched on at the same time. To make a long story short, the Murray D. Van Wagoner Bridge stands today as strong as ever over the Silver Creek in Morenci, Michigan. An orphaned metal truss has found a new home right beside it, and the town's people continue to observe their annual bridge walk, only now over two bridges.

The point of this story is simple. If restoration project decisions are made by only one person, the solution will reflect the point of view of that person. In the case of the Murray D. Van Wagoner Bridge, had the railing issue been left only to the engineer, the historic railing may not have survived. The engineer's solution would have been a proper solution, and it would have worked. However, it would have represented only one perspective in a much larger community of thought. When engineers collaborate with historians or contractors or, better yet, the steel fabricators who will actually be doing steel fabrication work, the ultimate preservation solution will reflect a much wiser and collective point of view. This is exactly what happened at the Murray D. Van Wagoner Bridge. Because the project began as a team effort and grew as a team effort through every stage of the restoration project, remarkable things happened.

Officials at the DOT and the SHPO were so impressed with how this project was managed that they brought the group together to develop a model for dealing with all historic bridge preservation throughout the state, especially of metal-truss bridges. These guidelines, or, as some would now call them, standard operating procedures for preserving historic metal-truss bridges in Michigan, recommend that a preservation team:

- Assemble a complete project team before engaging in any substantive design or repair work.
- Use team members (management, design, and construction) with experience in historical preservation.
- Use contract workers who are certified for restoration work, such as AWS-certified welders and knowledgeable steel fabricators.
- Rely on established practices that have been proven over time, such as regional painting protocols.
- Test restoration ideas before committing to them. For example, paint a small section of the bridge and evaluate its visual impact before the whole town shows up and says, "Egads, who picked that color?"
- Develop in advance a "technical work plan" from which to solicit meaningful bids, something detailed enough to clarify standards but not so excessively detailed that it inhibits creative solutions during the restoration process.
- Establish bidding procedures that do not bind the project team to the lowest bid. This acknowledges that bridge restoration work is more than a nuts-and-bolts proposition.
- Trust but verify all recommendations. In other words, never rely on any one point of view.

A point of view may be correct, but it may not be complete. A point of view may generate a good solution, but it may not generate the best solution. Never disparage a point of view. At the same time, never rely on just one point of view. Whether you are an engineer, a historian, or someone who holds the purse strings, take pride in your opinion, but listen carefully to all points of view.

One Final Note

Not too long ago, a small group of people was successful in securing a grant to preserve a bridge. Everything seemed to be going just fine until the project went over budget by $50,000. In the course of the construction work, the city manager had moved to another town. The new city manager was not as preservation-friendly. The makeup of the city commission also had changed, and the new commissioners, contending with other budget shortfalls, did not place much value on the languishing bridge project. "This is not our problem," they said. "Let the people who came up with the crazy idea deal . with it." Suffice it to say, the bridge project eventually was completed successfully.

Securing a bona fide constituency for your preservation project is not only helpful, it is absolutely necessary. Grant applications will ask for more than an enthusiastic show of hands; they will require affidavits of support, formal resolutions from your city or township commission, written contracts between agencies directly and indirectly affected by your bridge, and sometimes letters of guarantee from financial institutions. Gestures of goodwill may be inspirational, but they will not be enough to ensure that a preservation project succeeds. Broad-based support (in writing) from the leaders and civil servants of your community is essential.

CHAPTER 3

Raising Money

ike the politician who steadily recruits volunteers for a campaign or the salesperson who persistently makes phone calls for a monthly quota, he who would receive must ask. Obviously, one must have a worthy idea and be reasonably adept at expressing that idea both on paper and face-to-face with potential benefactors. One must also be prepared to accept occasional rejection, which may occur when the priorities of the asking organization are mismatched with the priorities of the giving organization or simply when budgets are tight. Nevertheless, in spite of the challenge of articulating your need and bracing for some inevitable rejections, the number one reason organizations come up short at fund-raising is simply that they don't ask. This chapter is about asking—whom to ask, how to ask, when to ask, why to ask, and what to ask for.

Ask big. Home-spun fund-raisers, such as car washes, bake sales, and bingo games, are great for creating a buzz around town. They can generate a little cash as well. However, they will never be able to raise the amount of money necessary to restore a bridge. If you are serious about saving your old bridge, you must turn to larger sources of funding. You must ask big.

Start with four major sources of funding: (1) the federal transportation enhancement program, (2) the federal critical bridge program, (3) county or city transportation organizations, and (4) local corporate and personal philanthropic funding sources.

Enhancement Funding

The largest single source of funding for the restoration of historic bridges is the federal enhancement program first enacted by Congress in 1991 and continued in subsequent years (see ISTEA in appendix 2). Embedded in this act of Congress is a provision stipulating that each state must set aside a minimum of 10 percent of its federal transportation dollars for projects that improve the quality of transportation life in the state—hence the word *enhancement*. Enhancement money may be used for a wide variety of transportation-related projects, such as building pedestrian or bike trails, restoring historic transportation buildings, or rehabilitating historic bridges. In Michigan, annual enhancement funding exceeds $20 million. Not bad for a beautification budget.

Each state department of transportation establishes guidelines for awarding enhancement funds. In Michigan, for example, enhancement funds pay up to 80 percent of a project's construction costs. The applicant must pay 20 percent of construction costs plus all engineering and design costs. Sometimes project proposals have a better chance of competing for funding if the applicant puts up more than a 20 percent match for the federal money.

Do not rush to the conclusion that enhancement funds will pay for most of your preservation project. What initially appears to be an 80 percent grant turns out to be a 52 percent stipend after the small-print restrictions have been applied. Check with your state's department of transportation for the rules, procedures, and deadlines for applying for enhancement funds.

Critical Bridge Funding

The critical bridge program is another source of funding that may be used for the restoration of historic bridges. It is a provision of STURAA, the Surface Transportation and Uniform Relocation Assistance Act of 1987 (see appendix 2). Critical bridge funds are not as plentiful or as flexible as enhancement

Table 1. Sample Bridge Budget

TYPE OF WORK	COST	ENHANCEMENT FUNDS	CRITICAL BRIDGE FUNDS
Consultation	$30,000	$0	$0
Engineering and design	$50,000	$0	$0
Construction	$150,000	$120,000	$30,000
TOTAL PROJECT COST	$230,000	($120,000 + $30,000) 65%*	

*A balance of $80,000 (35%) must be raised through other sources.

Table 2. Project Cost Breakdowns

PROJECT	FEDERAL & STATE FUNDING	LOCAL FUNDING	TOTAL PROJECT COST
Bridge Street Bridge	$182,000	$136,000	$318,000
Portland, Michigan	57%	43%	
Sixth Street Bridge	$265,000	$176,000	$441,000
Grand Rapids, Michigan	60%	40%	
McKeown Road Bridge	$48,233	$41,087	$89,320
Barry County, Michigan	54%	46%	
57th Avenue Bridge	$598,219	$149,554	$747,773
Allegan County, Michigan	80%	20%	

funds. They are limited to the would-be demolition costs of the bridge and in some states can be used to restore only state-owned bridges.

Like the enhancement program, the critical bridge fund requires preservation teams to match federal dollars with state and local money. In Michigan, a 15 percent match is required from the state, and 5 percent is required from the local community when critical bridge funds are used. This means that to secure $30,000 of critical bridge funds for the restoration of a bridge, the state would need to add $5,625, and the local community would need to raise $1,875, for a total of $7,500.

Table 1 provides an example of a bridge budget, showing how different pots of money can contribute to a project. Table 2 shows percentage breakdowns from several actual preservation projects in Michigan that relied on both enhancement funding and critical bridge funding.

The moment federal or state dollars are used in a preservation project, strings become attached. The project must comply with federal transportation construction standards. Strict hiring and contracting protocols must be followed. Environmental reviews and archeological surveys must be conducted, and project specifications must be monitored and approved by the state historic preservation office. Do not become too disheartened by these strings. In the long run, they will make your project better. Besides, if you were giving away your money, you would attach a few strings, too.

If an organization hopes to tap into some of these federal and state dollars, it must be prepared to spend a good amount of time filling out grant applications. The task of completing these many-page documents can be formidable but is achievable even for the smallest of communities. We will review the grant-writing process later in this chapter. For now, realize that enhancement funds and critical bridge funds are ready and waiting to be used for historic bridge preservation. Ask for them. If you don't, someone else will.

Occasionally, a community will be able to underwrite the entire cost of a bridge preservation project without relying on federal or state funds. Such was the case with the citizens of Barton Village, Michigan, as they worked to restore their 119-foot Pratt through truss (1876), locally called the Foster Bridge but in broader Michigan circles known as Maple Road Bridge over the Huron River. The people of Barton Village were able to support a good portion of the project financially, and the road commission also was able to pitch in some funds for the project. Add to this a large donation from an anonymous donor, and the old Foster Bridge was well on its way to a new life. This is indeed a rare scenario, as bridge preservation budgets usually far exceed a local community's ability to pay for them. But when funding is local and complete, the preservation team enjoys a greater degree of flexibility in its work. Still guided by state laws and AASHTO standards, the preservation team may consider creative solutions in process and design, as state and federal guidelines (strings) are not attached.

County or City Transportation Funding

Local government agencies annually budget funds for bridge construction, maintenance, and repair. Under special circumstances, these line-item resources may be tapped for preservation projects. You will need someone on the inside to lobby for this type of budget funding. So don't forget to recruit a city or county official on your preservation team.

Local Funding

The admonition to ask big applies not only to soliciting government funds but also to seeking local business and personal philanthropic support. Many large sources of funding may be right within your own hometown. Local engineering and construction companies may view your request as a perfect platform from which to tout their services. Area foundations may identify with your philosophical goals. Wealthy residents may find your request to be just the right cause to spice up their philanthropic lives.

The Ditch Road Bridge had stood over the Shiawassee River in Saginaw County for more than 100 years. In an attempt to save this rare Thacher through truss, the community of Chesaning, Michigan, devised a plan to move it to a city park in the center of town and use it as a pedestrian bridge. The only problem with this great idea was that it was going to cost $385,000, a pretty hefty price for the small town. Even with enhancement and critical bridge funds, the community needed to raise $125,000 locally.

It took some time, but the folks of Chesaning rallied the troops and were able to secure several major pledges from both businesses and nonprofit groups, along with more than half a dozen personal gifts of $1,000 plus several in-kind donations of materials and labor.

General Ideas about Fund-raising

■ Pull together a team. The larger, the better. The likelihood of success for any public endeavor is directly proportional to the number of people and organizations involved in the project. This is especially true for fund-raising.

Table 3. The Community of Chesaning Matching Fund-raising Campaign

$30,000	Showboat Theater Group
$5,000	Saginaw Community Foundation
$10,000	Harvey Randal Wicks Foundation
$2,500	Wickson-Link Foundation
$40,800	Sponsorship of bridge deck planks with commemorative plates
$12,700	Other sources
$24,000	Yet to be secured
$125,000	Local match

- Put together a plan. Clearly articulate (on paper) how much money you need, how it will be used, and why an individual or organization should give it to you.
- Brainstorm potential benefactors. Leave no stone unturned.
- All donations count. Be ambitious, and seek out the $5,000 ones, but don't forget the $50 ones.
- Personal visits are always better than mail solicitation. There is a time for mail solicitation but only after personal visits have been exhausted. Show up face-to-face, and people will reward you for your time and courage.
- Never forget the power of posterity. Chesaning raised more than $40,000 by selling the opportunity to have its citizens' names engraved on brass nameplates on the bridge planks for $200 each.
- Involve the media. Sponsor a songwriting contest about the bridge, to be aired over the local radio station with a $50 entrance fee. Ask the local newspaper to sponsor an essay contest about the importance of historic preservation. Don't forget the entrance fee.
- Involve young people. Have the high school choir record a collection of songs about bridges and sell their CD as a fund-raising project. Youth service clubs have energy to spare when it comes to taking on a cause.
- Play on nostalgia. Publish and sell photographs of the bridge—framed or printed on plates, Christmas ornaments, or T-shirts.
- Don't forget raffles, barbecue dinners, and, of course, bingo games. There

are many ways to raise money locally. Take the time to brainstorm ideas that fit the character and temperament of your community. Always remember that the likelihood of success for any public endeavor is directly proportional to the number of people and organizations involved.

Grant Applications

Applying for a grant is like watching a scary movie. The first time through, you are likely to crouch in the corner of your couch, peering at the screen through a pillow pulled up around your head. During the second viewing, you are less frightened but still flinch at the scary parts. By the third time, you kick your feet up on the coffee table and wonder, "Why was I ever afraid in the first place?" Applying for a grant can be intimidating, but just like watching a scary movie, the more you do it, the less frightening it becomes. No one knows this better than Margaret Barondess.

When I first talked with Margaret Barondess on the phone, it was easy to conjure images of a woman living in a large English manor with an entrance lined by honey locust trees. With a name like Barondess, she must be royalty, I was sure. When I finally met her in her office, my image of the British highlands had subsided, but I was still equally impressed. Her walls were filled with transportation maps, bridge photos, and schematics of community bike trails. The top of her desk seemed purposefully cluttered with just the right number of working papers and sticky notes, all hedged in by three-ring binders and books, including a *Bridges of the World* coloring book. Margaret Barondess is significant to this story because she is one of the key people at MDOT who reviews enhancement grant applications. If you're hoping to secure federal funding in Michigan, you've got to talk to Margaret.

"How many enhancement grant proposals have you reviewed?" I asked, to get the conversation going. "Hundreds." she said. "No, thousands," she added, correcting herself with laughter. "At least, it seems like thousands."

Margaret has seen many funding requests for preserving bridges, rehabilitating historic railroad depots, converting abandoned rail easements to bike trails, and even simple roadside landscaping schemes. "We'll consider almost anything, as long as it has some tie to transportation."

"What do you typically look for in an application?" I asked.

"Most grant application forms ask three questions," she said. "How much money do you want? What is the money going to be used for? And why should we give it to you?"

Despite the many questions and line-by-line budget justifications that grant applications call for, it seems that the people who review them are really looking for one thing: clarity. She phrased it another way: "Read the directions, skip the hyperbole, and get to the point."

"The things that some people say in these applications can be downright comical," she continued without coaxing. "When asked to explain the benefits of the project to the community, one applicant suggested that the new bridge would all but fight poverty, reduce intergenerational tensions, and eliminate crime, and all this was presented in romance-novel form." Laughter came from one of her colleagues in the office next door, who confirmed the story and began to tell a few tales of his own. "Don't get me wrong." Margaret Barondess said. "We welcome passionate presentations, but mostly we just want to know: How much money do you need? What is it going to be used for? And why should we give it to you?"

Margaret Barondess's directness was refreshing and not in the least disrespectful. This was serious business. Each year, she and her MDOT colleagues are charged with dispersing $20 million to make Michigan a more attractive state. She and her team are prepared to give every application a fair and thorough hearing.

"How long does it typically take a preservation group to fill out an enhancement application?" I asked.

"A couple of weeks, at least. The time is needed not so much for writing but rather for gathering information."

"What kind of information?"

Margaret opened a file drawer, thumbed her way through an array of color-coordinated hanging folders, and pulled out a 1992 enhancement application from the city of Portland, Michigan.

The Portland community turned to enhancement funding to expand its city trail system. The project included a pedestrian pathway (for hiking, jogging, and biking), a canoe launch, an area for parking, lighting, and the rehabilitation of two metal-truss bridges that would be used at critical connecting points on the trail. The budget for the entire project came to approximately \$900,000 (\$515,000 from the enhancement program and \$385,000 from local sources). The cost for the two bridge projects (one a Warren pony truss and the other a Pratt through truss) included a \$318,000 enhancement request plus a local match of \$136,000. We spent the next few minutes looking through the thirty-page document.

The grant application was divided into three sections. The first requested the most basic of information and was easily completed within a minute or two. The second section included a checklist to determine what category of funding the project related to most. Likewise, this section was quite easy to complete. Note Portland's response to the categories below.

NONMOTORIZED
- ✔ Provision of facilities for pedestrians and bicycles
- ✔ Preservation of abandoned railway corridors

TRANSPORTATION AESTHETICS
- ✘ Scenic highway programs
- ✘ Acquisition of scenic easements and scenic sites
- ✘ Landscaping and other scenic beautification
- ✘ Control and removal of outdoor advertising

MITIGATION
- ✘ Mitigation of water pollution due to highway runoff

HISTORIC PRESERVATION
- ✘ Acquisition of historic sites
- ✔ Historic highway programs
- ✘ Historic preservation
- ✔ Rehabilitation and operation of historic transportation buildings, structures, or facilities (including railroad facilities and canals)
- ✘ Archaeological planning and research

The heart of the grant application came in its third section, which requested information about the organization seeking the funds, the nature of the project, budget projections, and the benefits of the project to the community. Now, this was the hard part.

- Describe your organization and its interest in the proposed project.
- Describe the existing transportation facility and the proposed work (include photographs as may be appropriate).
- Provide a formal description of the project's location (include maps).
- Evidence of eligibility.
- Complete an environmental review.
- Calculations and working papers to support budget.
- Benefits of proposed project.
- Implementation schedule.
- Resolutions of support from local units of government.
- Proposed maintenance plans, agreements, and preservation covenants.

Margaret was quick to point out, "Don't think that a layperson needs to know all the answers to these questions. That is what consultants are for."

"So it is the consultant who writes the grant?" I asked skeptically.

"The completing of an enhancement grant application is usually the collaborative work of several individuals. It is rare for any one layperson—or professional, for that matter—to be able to do it," she answered.

I left Margaret Barondess's office that day with an assignment to review thirty pages of rationale for why MDOT should award $515,000 to the City of Portland. I have included Portland's answers to some of the questions above in appendix 3 to provide a sense of how one community tackled the task of grant writing.

Whether you are seeking federal, state, or local funding, you will be required to articulate your request on paper. Grant writing can be an intimidating task. When stumped, ask for help. Turn the technical stuff over to the consultants and engineers, and heed these summary words of advice:

- Start early. If you think you are going to sit at your kitchen table on Sunday afternoon and be ready to mail the grant by Monday morning, you're in for a big surprise. I've seen college term papers quiver in the shadow of a well-completed enhancement grant application.
- Work as a team. Two heads are better than one, especially if they are smart heads. Having more than one person working on the grant also should keep everyone's spirit high.

- Answer questions directly. Give specific reasons or examples to bolster your point.
- Be honest. Don't underestimate. Don't exaggerate. Those reviewing your application will be able to see through your puffing.
- Demonstrate a broad community of support for the project. Points will be deducted if the application sounds as if it is coming from just one or two people.
- Double-check for last-minute details, such as number of copies, proper mailing address, and postmark deadline. Make sure the format of your presentation is precisely what was called for. For example, should the pages be three-hole-punched or stapled?
- Enjoy the feeling of accomplishment when you close the manila envelope and drop the completed application in the mail.

CHAPTER 4

Understanding the Role of the Consultant-Engineer

As Al Halbeisen led me to his office on the lower level of his home, I could not help but notice some hair barrettes, school papers, and a backpack—a dead giveaway to a place normally energized with children. I also detected an uncommon assortment of framed metal-truss bridge pictures mixed in with family photos, increasing in number as we got closer to his office. I had been told he was a bit shy but, without question, one of the most highly respected bridge consultants in the state. I was eager to talk to Al Halbeisen.

"So, tell me," I asked teasingly, to break the ice, "what exactly does a bridge consultant do?"

Al Halbeisen chuckled. "I ask myself that very question quite often."

His laughter confirmed that we were off to a good start.

Consultants are often portrayed as overrated, overpriced, necessary evils for projects technically beyond mortal laypeople. In the bridge preservation business, nothing could be farther from the truth. A good consultant can perform miracles on what may appear to be a bridge without a chance. His or her fees may add 10 to 15 percent to the project budget, but the value he or she adds will be worth the cost. A good consultant will not only answer questions, he or she will also raise questions that may not have been considered. A good consultant will not only assess the technical condition of your bridge, but also explain in ordinary language the reason and process for each repair. He or she will create a detailed budget for your project and, equally important, reveal avenues for funding. Al Halbeisen seemed to be all of these things, and as we continued to talk, I kept thinking to myself, "If I were trying to save an old bridge, this is the kind of guy I'd like to have on my side."

"My first job is to listen." Al Halbeisen said. "I need to get a good sense of what the community wants and what it needs."

"What specifically do you listen for?"

"I try to determine the group's level of understanding of the problem; what it is they think they can accomplish, what options they may have already considered. I also try to get a sense of the makeup of the group—who is involved, what roles do they play, what particular interests do they have?"

"What can you uniquely offer to such a group?" I continued.

"The company I work for is an engineering company, so we are able to bring a strong engineering background to any historic restoration project. We can assess the condition of their bridge and manage the construction project for them, if they desire."

I came to understand that some consultants specialize in history, some in metal fabrication, still others in fund-raising. These focused experts can indeed be helpful to your cause, but because bridge preservation is a highly technical undertaking, there is no substitute for a consultant who is also an engineer. The real challenge is to find one who has an appreciation for historic bridges as well as a demonstrated technical understanding of them.

In moderate to large-size cities, you can find such consultants in the yellow pages of the phone book. Most Internet search engines will spew out more names than can be meaningfully digested in a lifetime. The best place to turn to is your state department of transportation. State officials are typically not allowed to recommend one firm over another, but they can provide a list of consulting organizations with which they regularly do business. This in itself is a good clue to a firm's reputation. Your department of transportation also will be able to give you the names and phone numbers of communities in your state that have recently done bridge restoration work. Their recommendations should be trustworthy.

"What qualities should one be looking for in a consultant-engineer?" I asked, hoping that Al Halbeisen would not be too modest.

He warmed up my coffee and then leaned back in his chair and began to talk more reflectively about the characteristics of a good consultant. I have distilled his comments into four short bits of advice: insist on someone with credentials; look for someone who has experience in restoring metal-truss bridges; seek out someone with an open mind; and find a good listener.

Credentials

The consultant-engineer should be licensed as a professional engineer specializing in either civil or structural engineering. A consultant need not be part of a large organization. A small consulting group or even a solitary entrepreneur may be the right match for you. Whatever the organizational status of the consultant, insist on credentials.

Experience

An engineering firm may boast an army of consultants renowned for their work on reinforced concrete spans, but if the firm does not employ people who have worked on metal trusses, it will be mismatched to your project, no matter how famous it is. Metal-truss bridge restoration presents unique engineering, historical, and aesthetic challenges. It is important to seek out those who can actually show you pictures of past metal-truss projects they have worked on, who can review with you case studies they have already completed, who have been so engaged in bringing a metal-truss bridge back to life that they even hang framed pictures of successes on the walls of their homes.

An Open Mind

Engineers by training are required to play it safe. If it were not for their methodical, cautious, fail-safe way of doing things, the world of transportation would be a precarious one indeed. Having an open mind is not about cutting corners with safety. It is a willingness to look at restoration challenges from more than a textbook point of view. It is about having professional courage to explore options that may not have been considered before. Consultant-engineers must demonstrate an uncompromising respect for safety, but if you are lucky, you will find one who also is willing to value the historic and aesthetic qualities of your bridge.

A Good Listener

We have all encountered at one time or another self-confident verbal locomotives who seem to know what is best for everyone even before the introductory pleasantries are over. Beware of such quick-to-speak and slow-to-listen advisors. They will burden your efforts.

Professional graciousness usually accompanies a good consultant. Call it unpretentious confidence or just good manners; whatever the name, this character trait is as important as the ability to calculate load ratings or run stress formulas. The consultant must do more than simply answer questions. He or she must be capable of guiding local leaders through the peaks and pitfalls of preservation work and have a good working relationship with state officials. He or she must bring wisdom to the team, and, equally important, he or she should contribute a sense of enthusiasm to the project.

Al Halbeisen and I continued to talk about the various characteristics of the ideal consultant until I interrupted with a bit of sarcasm: "What are the realistic prospects of ever hiring such a perfect person?"

"It's not unreasonable to request meetings with several candidates. The initial meeting between the consultant and the preservation group often takes place at the bridge."

"What types of questions do you usually encounter at this initial get-together?"

- What is your general assessment of our bridge? Can it be saved?
- What do we need to do to get the process going?
- Have you or your firm ever helped in restoring a bridge like this before?
- Will you be able to give us some direction or assistance in securing funds for this project?
- How do we go about bringing you formally onboard?

"I suppose they will eventually need to know how much your services cost," I injected.

He smiled. "That certainly comes up."

A consultant will also want to ask the preservation group some questions:

- Why are you undertaking this project? What are your motivations?
- What do you know about the bridge so far?
- What input have you received from your department of transportation and your state historic preservation office?
- What plans or options have you considered for the bridge? Will it be used for vehicular or pedestrian traffic?
- To what degree of historical accuracy do you hope to restore the bridge?
- How much community support do you have for this project?

At the request of the group, the consultant will provide a general proposal for assisting with the project. This proposal will not reveal how much it will cost to restore your bridge. Instead, it will outline the process and cost for putting together a detailed preservation plan. In implementing this preservation plan, a total project budget will slowly emerge. The initial proposal will outline the responsibilities of the consulting firm, a timeline of activities, rates for services, and general agreement on how the consultant and the preservation project team will work together. If accepted, a formal contract will be signed, and the consultant will begin his or her work in earnest.

I was beginning to sense that Al Halbeisen was getting his second wind, so I said yes to his offer to warm up my cup of coffee again, and we both settled back for the part of the conversation best left for the next chapter.

CHAPTER 5

Assessing the Value, Preservation Options, and Condition of Your Bridge

Critique, not to be confused with criticism, is a liberating practice. All disciplines require it. All undertakings benefit from it, and preservation projects are no exception. This chapter is about bridge critique—the process of assessing the value, preservation options, and condition of your bridge.

Assessing the Value of Your Bridge

The average old metal-truss bridge weighs approximately forty tons. Scrap iron is worth only pennies per pound. Do the math, and you will quickly see that if an old bridge is to merit preservation, its value must be equal to more than the sum of its disposable parts. It value must be understood as its worthiness as a bridge plus its added value as a historic structure, an engineering marvel, an educational time capsule, and sometimes a work of art.

The rarer a bridge design is, the more valuable it is. The 57th Street Bridge of Allegan, Michigan, was not only a rare swing-span pony truss, it was a hand-cranked, one-man-operated, swing-span pony truss! Bridge historians could locate nothing else like it. The ability to document unique aspects of its design made the 57th Street Bridge priceless to the Allegan community.

A variety of public records were found for the State Street Bridge in Saginaw County, Michigan. Minutes of township meetings, financial statements, photographs, and even placards posted on trees to bid out the construction process provided a portfolio of ammunition for the preservation cause.

Registering a bridge on the State or National Register of Historic Places requires careful notation of its design and structural peculiarities and meticulous listing of noteworthy events throughout its life. By connecting your bridge to the significant people and colorful events of its past, you will actually increase its value as a community asset.

An old bridge is like a first source document that when read carefully, reveals much about its past. Its rivets, its metallurgy, its design and ornamentation—all give us clues about the people and circumstances around which it was made. In other words, old bridges have something to teach us. Like a detective at a crime scene, a bridge scholar can command a silent bridge to speak simply by asking the right questions. "Why were these particular rivets used?" "Where did this unusual metal come from?" "How did they ever get this thing here in the first place?" Historians read books; archeologists study steel. In the same way we value the paper archives of our local library, communities can rightly value their rusty bridge as a first source document.

Once in a while, a bridge will achieve prominence not because of its history or design but simply because of its setting. The St. Joseph River winds its way some 200 miles through what used to be prime hunting ground for the Potawatomi, a Native American tribe. Today, at the highest spot overlooking this Michigan river are remnants of a Potawatomi campground and an old iron bridge. Unspoiled by modern development, the bridge sits quietly between a cultural legacy and some of the most scenic river land in the Midwest. No one would seek to destroy this bridge any more than they would want to cut down the 175-year-old linden tree visible from its deck. The setting is just too aesthetically wonderful.

In 1990, the Portland Bridge Street Bridge, an 1890 rare two-span through truss over the Grand River, was on the docket for repair or replacement.

The Bridge Street Bridge over the Grand River in the small town of Portland, just east of Grand Rapids, was rehabilitated in 1990, kicking off a local enthusiasm for truss bridge preservation that continues today. Portland has gone on to repair an old railroad truss and moved two other trusses to serve the local bike path system.

During the first round of deliberations, advocates for new construction cited structural problems, while preservationists countered with estimates and options of their own. Back and forth, strategies were bantered, and when all the fiscal dust had settled, the leaders of the community realized that by converting the bridge to one-way traffic to accommodate its structural limitations, they could rehabilitate it for modern traffic use. The community solved a transportation problem, preserved a defining monument of their town, and saved money, too, by understanding the value of their bridge as a bridge.

This last example is important, because most old bridges will ultimately be saved, not for poetic value but rather out of sheer financial will. It is the bottom line that will ultimately determine the real value of your bridge.

Assessing the Preservation Options of Your Bridge

The National Transportation Act of 1966 and the National Historic Preservation Act of the same year provide guidelines and incentives to communities for preserving historic bridges (see appendix 2). Charles K. Hyde's book *Historic Highway Bridges of Michigan* identifies five fundamental options.

Live and Let Live

If a bridge is tucked away down a seldom-traveled country road, and if it is, for all practical purposes, no longer needed, the community may allow it to remain in place as an artifact of its environment. As long as safety issues have been addressed and the bridge is fundamentally sound, simply leaving it alone is a preservation option in itself. The only Queen Post truss in Michigan stands quietly over a very small creek (more like a large ditch) in Clinton County. Its entrance is blocked to any vehicle that might try to cross it, but every now and then, it comes in handy for the Sunday afternoon hiker.

Another closed-off road in Clinton County leads up to a 125-foot Parker truss. This bridge crosses the Maple River at a spillway and naturally frames a man-made waterfall and lake popular with local anglers. From a distance, its profile appears as clean and stunning as it was on the day it was inaugurated. Up close, it is easy to see that this bridge has been weathered by time. Its entrances have been closed off to vehicles, but its deck and railing remain adequate for pedestrian traffic.

Living Side by Side

Some bridges can be left in place while traffic is rerouted to a new location, often within sight of the original bridge. This preservation option is uncommon because of limited availability of land, inevitable road alignment problems, and the redundant cost of maintaining two bridges side by side. Four examples of this type of parallel coexistence are found in Michigan. Three

Michigan's only Queen Post truss can be found in Clinton County on a winding country road. Some years ago, the road commission bypassed this small truss with a more modern road. Without the corrosive effects of salt, it may last a long time here.

are metal-truss bridges, and one is a concrete arch. All are now pedestrian bridges.

The McKeown Road Bridge over the Thornapple River in Barry County, Michigan, became a pedestrian crossing while cars zoomed by on the new bridge less than 300 feet away. The Eagle River Bridge also parallels its successor. It was virtually impossible to relocate the old bridge, because it was a deck-truss bridge that had been especially designed for a specific place. A rare three-span camelback bridge in Mottville, Michigan, likewise remained the center focus of town as thousands of cars passed daily over the new bridge very close to its side. It had been impossible to widen and impossible to move. If this historic bridge were to survive, coexistence was the only option. Finding a parallel route over the river actually improved the flow of traffic for this major trunk line from Detroit to Chicago. Forty miles east on the same highway that the Mottville Bridge served lies a small Warren pony

Aaron T. Brodeur

Federal enhancement funds helped preserve the McKeown Road Bridge for pedestrian use. Road officials replaced it with a newer bridge, but citizens wanted to save the old bridge. A nearby senior citizens home benefits from access to the bridge.

truss, which by its unique location doubles as an entrance to the city and also as the front door to the town cemetery. Today, this little fifteen-foot-wide pony truss lies dormant next to its four-lane, steel-reinforced-concrete big brother fifty yards away.

Rehabilitate for Original Use

Of all the options available to the preservationist, rehabilitating an old bridge to remain in place as a working bridge for cars may be the most difficult one of all. Not only must the bridge be repaired, its rust removed, its damaged members fixed, its camber restored, and all of its metal primed and painted, but it must also be brought up to code. Heavier guardrails may be needed. The truss itself may require reinforcement with extra diagonals or substruts and ties. Stronger material may need to be used for the deck. Load levels may need to be posted.

Bridges built before 1920 are almost always too narrow for today's two-lane traffic, and widening a through truss is a complicated and expensive

This Warren truss in Coldwater is showing its age. The state highway department bypassed it years ago, before federal legislation required federal aid project planners to consider impacts on historic resources. Now that it is a local bridge, its repair may not compete well with other priorities in the community.

proposition. The community of Allegan, Michigan, solved this problem by putting a stoplight at each entrance of its 1898 bridge so that traffic could take turns crossing. Not only did this provide plenty of room for vehicles, but it also reduced the overall load levels on the bridge. This solution may not work at every location. However, it is an idea to consider seriously if you need the bridge for vehicular traffic. Turning an old two-lane bridge into a one-lane, one-way bridge, perhaps even with posted load levels, can keep it in service for a long time.

Rehabilitating a nineteenth-century bridge to accommodate twenty-first-century traffic may indeed be difficult. It is, however, doable and sometimes less expensive than starting from scratch. The 2nd Street Bridge of Allegan is a perfect example. To replace this 1886 Pratt truss would have cost $1.5 million. To rehabilitate it would be $500,000, three times less expensive.

Many times, it is cheaper to tear down an old metal truss and replace it with a simple wooden or steel-reinforced-concrete beam bridge. Sometimes, though, it is not. A wise evaluation must consider both current-day construction costs and long-term maintenance and repair costs.

Relocate

Of all the many different types of bridges, such as stone, wood, metal, or concrete, metal-truss bridges are the most amenable to relocation. Some of the smaller ones can even be picked up in one piece and transported on a flatbed truck or even carried by helicopter. If they are too large to be moved in one piece, they can be taken apart and hauled to their new homes. The Federal Highway Administration encourages this preservation option by providing funding for relocation equivalent to what demolition costs would have been. (For more details about these monies see the Surface Transportation and Uniform Relocation Assistance Act in appendix 2.)

The Calhoun County Historic Bridge Park

Some call it a bridge orphanage. Others think of it as a truss retirement home. Most know it best as the Calhoun County Historic Bridge Park. No other public park dedicated solely to showcasing historic metal-truss bridges exists in the United States. It is indeed a one-of-a-kind bridge relocation phenomenon. Located a few miles southeast of Battle Creek just off I-94 where the interstate crosses the Kalamazoo River, this five-acre parcel of land currently is home to four metal-truss bridges that have been collected from throughout Michigan. More are on their way. It is a wonderful place for a Sunday afternoon walk over, around, and under old metal-truss bridges.

Things to Do If All Else Fails

If preservation efforts have been exhausted and communities conclude that demolition is the best choice, then thorough documentation of the bridge is recommended (required if federal money is involved) before it is taken down.

Formal guidelines for this documentation are outlined in the Historic American Engineering Record (HAER), available through the National Park Service. The HAER report form asks that you complete a narrative about your bridge, compile a bibliography of all source material used in documenting

The Calhoun County Historic Bridge Park is a unique collection of truss bridges. The process of creating the park has fostered the development of repair techniques benefiting bridges throughout the nation.

it, and create a graphic record of your project. This visual record could be an album of hand-drawn sketches, photographs, or videographic images of your bridge. Copies of the HAER report are then kept in various local and state archives and also at the Library of Congress.

Demolition does not have to be as final as the word suggests. There are creative ways to honor the memory of a bridge that no longer can be used for traffic. The portal of its truss may be serve as an entranceway into a park. A side may be mounted on a brick wall as an exterior decoration. Critical pieces may be saved as spare parts for other restoration projects. Much of the bridge may be donated to the local community college welding department with an assignment: "Be artfully creative, and learn something about welding old metal while you're at it." Before you go hauling away that old iron skeleton to the scrap heap, give it one more chance at life through creative reuse.

Assessing the Condition of Your Bridge

All things under stress get tired after a while, and metal is no exception. Metal fatigue is an inevitable wearing out of a bridge on a molecular level because of the day-to-day stresses it has endured throughout its life. Tired metal in a bridge can be a problem. However, because the process of fatigue takes such a long time to appear, a variety of other problems will surface long before general fatigue threatens a bridge's life. No one has been able to point to a bridge that was condemned simply because it was old.

Rust is a fact of bridge life, and those in the bridge business will readily tell you that you just have to deal with it. But just how do you deal with it? When is rust a superficial nuisance that a good wire brushing and a fresh coat of paint will take care of, and when does it become deadly? These questions must be answered on a case-by-case basis by experts. Generally speaking, though, if more than 5 percent of the cross section of metal has been oxidized, you've got a serious problem.

Rust can vanquish a half-inch-thick piece of unprotected steel in a relatively short period of time. That same piece of metal, if kept painted and cleaned, will last indefinitely. The very first metal bridge, built in 1779 in Coalbrookdale, England, continues to stand today primarily because it was taken care of. A neglected metal-truss bridge, on the other hand, can perish in a generation.

Early metal bridges in this country did not rust as readily as their twentieth-century cousins, because their metal contained a high level of phosphorus, a common rust-inhibiting impurity in early iron and steel. This element, removed from structural steel in the mid-1920s to make bridge steel more ductile and easier to weld, was the primary reason many old trusses have survived as well as they have until today.

Iron was indeed a revolutionary building material that allowed bridges to be lighter and carry heavier loads, but iron did not immunize bridges from physical damage caused by excess loads or inattentive drivers. Bent vertical posts, buckled cover plates, the separation of forge-welded eyebars—why are these seemingly minor defects such big problems in the bridge business? Consider the following engineering primer.

The triangle is the ubiquitous engineering form that makes all bridges work. (How many triangles can you count in the Warren truss photo on page

ABOVE: The 20 Mile Road Bridge in the Calhoun County Historic Bridge Park shows how various-sized triangles work together to form a truss.

LEFT: Rust continually expands, pushing its way into any available space, bending metal and seizing up joints. This photo shows pack rust that has formed between the I-bar and a vertical member on the Marantette Bridge.

Aaron T. Brodeur

When structural supports get damaged, the truss works poorly.

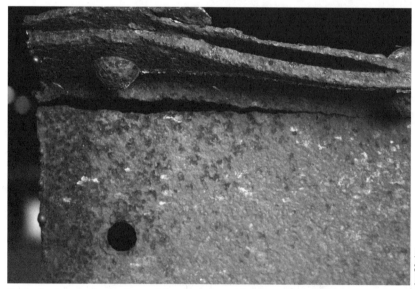

Cracks develop over time and are a serious sign of metal fatigue.

45?) If a primary element of any truss (a side of a triangle) is bent, then the force being transferred from one point to another (through compression or tension) is interrupted, or at least redirected, and the effectiveness of the truss is compromised.

The buckling of a plate from rust, a vertical post dented by a wayward car—these minor bends or wobbles may not seem critical to the layperson, but under more careful scrutiny, they are no longer triangles, and they significantly degrade the integrity of the truss. When the fundamental form of the truss (the triangle) has been damaged, the integrity of the bridge is compromised. That is why all structural damage to a bridge, except for cosmetic ornamentation, must be repaired. There is a reason for all those triangles, and they need to be straight. (Procedures for straightening elements of a truss are discussed in chapter 8.)

What may appear to the casual observer to be a riverworthy truss may to the trained eye be a span riddled with an engineer's nightmare: cracks. Caused most often by excess stress from heavier and heavier traffic over the years, cracks are like a slow-growing cancer that will surely decommission an otherwise healthy bridge. A bridge inspector worth his or her weight in bridge salt will know this and certainly be on the lookout for cracks. I've seen some hands-on inspectors actually scale a bridge like Curious George with a magnifying glass looking for them. Whether you inspect a bridge on location or examine it piece by piece in the shop, every square inch of metal must be checked for cracks.

How does one find tiny cracks sometimes invisible to the eye? Dye penetration and ultrasound are two effective techniques. We will talk more about these procedures later in this chapter.

The designs of most nineteenth- and early-twentieth-century bridges are woefully inadequate for today's traffic. A horse and buggy with a family of four on their way to church weighed about 2,500 pounds. A loaded UPS truck is ten times as heavy and twice as wide, to say nothing of the weight of a fire truck or a loaded moving van. The speed of vehicles has also greatly increased, mocking adages posted on many old bridge entranceways: "$5.00 fine for riding or driving on this bridge faster than a walk."

Outmoded design is one of the most difficult problems a preservation group will encounter, especially if the bridge is to remain in place for vehicular traffic. Bridges can be reinforced, and traffic can be limited to one

The Fallasburg covered bridge in Kent County still carries traffic, although no one collects the fine anymore. Many truss bridges had cautionary signs like this one.

way, but it is difficult to ask a bridge to carry an SUV when it was only designed for a Model A. The problem of antiquated design most often forces preservation groups to rethink location and use.

Transportation routes evolved to follow good ground lines—the natural contours of the land often associated with high ground or the course of a river. Metal was money, and building a bridge across the river in the shortest distance (at right angles to the bank) was the ideal. Therefore, many old bridges have approaches that abruptly turn into the bridge. This would not be a problem for a horse-drawn wagon, as they did not go very fast. Today's traffic, though, requires a little more advance notice.

The Indian Trail Road Bridge in St. Clair County, Michigan, is a good example of one such abrupt angle of approach. As 55-mile-per-hour traffic turned a bend, it was promptly met by a one-lane pony truss. Warning signs and speed limits were ineffective. Needless to say, this bridge has been moved, the road approaches have been straightened, and a reinforced-concrete bridge with a more accommodating skew across the river is now in place.

Nineteenth-century bridge builders were always looking for ways to save money. Consequently, many old metal-truss bridge abutments extended close to, and sometimes into, the water to reduce the length of the span. (Remember, the shorter the truss, the less expensive the bridge.) Unaware of modern-day theories of hydrology and riverbank conservation, and with no meaningful flood records to turn to, well-meaning masons, usually drafted from the local community, often created more problems than they solved. A quick spring thaw or a heavy rain would force the river up and around the abutments, undercutting them and scouring away their footing. Water turbulence from these man-made eddies could push a bridge off its abutments, causing it to sink immediately into the stream, or ice in wintertime could rip a bridge from its abutments, carrying it a hundred yards down the river like a runaway polar bear.

Abutments built on dry land and high enough to endure the uncommon flood are usually in manageable shape today and should require only repointing if they are made from stone or patching if they are made from concrete. However, most surviving abutments are usually out of code to

This Indiana bowstring truss bridge became a flood victim.

today's standards and need to be reconstructed farther away from the water's edge. Most highway agencies have adopted a standard that requires bridge abutments to be water-free up to a twenty-five-year flood level.

What happens when abutments are pulled back to meet today's construction standards and the bridge no longer fits? A small approach span, made of metal, wood, or concrete, can fill the gap between the new abutment and a post or pile in the river where the original abutments reached. Piles allow water to flow around them and may be permitted in rivers, but abutments are not.

Old, abandoned bridges are like jungle gyms for kids and roadside museums for grown-ups. They are an irresistible attraction for young and old alike. However, their charm creates a problem greater than any bent I-beam or rusted eyebar. It is one of safety and the consequent legal liability that comes with it.

It's a question that all preservation groups must answer: "What happens if someone gets hurt on our bridge?" Consider the following informal opinion offered by the Kansas attorney general's office, which has become a working model for historic bridge preservation projects across the nation:

> If an old bridge is built to acceptable standards for which it is being used,
> and if it is well maintained and free of safety problems, the bridge should
> not be a liability burden for its community.
>
> —Paul Daniel Marriot, *Saving Historic Roads: Design and Policy Guidelines,* 1998

This guideline seems to be quite reasonable, but note carefully all the qualifiers. How are "acceptable standards" determined? Who establishes the scope of a bridge's use? How are these use standards controlled over time? These questions, and others equally relevant, must be answered by the transportation authority under whose jurisdiction your old bridge will ultimately fall. However, more important to the issue of liability than any one of these answers will be the overall safety attitude that the responsible organization displays toward its bridges. How can an organization display an attitude? By articulating a comprehensive public safety policy for all of its bridges and by demonstrating a willingness to implement that policy over time. In other words, a well-thought-out safety plan that is followed is the best defense against liability claims.

Issues of safety and liability should not dissuade the preservationist from restoring an old bridge, for safety applies to all public structures, not just historic ones. Consequently, it doesn't matter if a bridge is old or new, there will always be risks in crossing a river.

Buildings need it, parks have it, and bridges can't live without it. It's called liability insurance, and no matter how well your bridge has been restored and is maintained, it will need to be insured. The cost for such insurance can be quite high, but the risk of not having it, especially for small communities, is unbearably higher. Sixty-five of the eighty-three counties in Michigan have managed this expense by forming an insurance alliance—a type of formal partnership that collectively spreads local transportation liability over the group. In so doing, individual authorities have been able to increase the liability coverage for their local bridges while reducing their overall insurance premiums. The rules of this alliance are simple. Each unit of government that is responsible for front-line bridge management (in Michigan, it is the county road commission) pays an annual premium to the alliance and is responsible for a modest deductible should a claim be awarded. Representatives of this alliance in turn negotiate with major insurance providers to underwrite the total alliance area. With the risk spread over a large group, the cost of insuring any one locale is significantly reduced. Each state is unique in how it organizes its transportation authorities. Whatever bureaucratic structure your state has adopted, providing liability insurance for your historic bridge is essential and should be well within reach.

A privately owned bridge is like the sword of Damocles dangling by a thread over its master's head. One false move, and you're done for. Unless you are unspeakably wealthy and can personally endure multi-million-dollar lawsuits or you have so sheltered your bridge from the public that it has become essentially useless, give it away as soon as possible. Bequeathing your bridge to a public authority or nonprofit trust will eliminate liability on your part and will allow you and the rest of the public to enjoy it for a long time.

The responsibility for an old bridge should not be taken lightly. As with any public structure, those who have been charged with its care must remain ever diligent. Practicing a well-thought-out safety plan is the first step in making your bridge secure. A good bridge insurance policy should take care of the rest.

A Bridge Study for Portland, Michigan

In an attempt to give our general discussion some real-life application, Al Halbeisen, our colleague from the previous chapter, directed my attention to an actual bridge assessment his company had completed for Portland, Michigan.

"Read through this carefully," he said, "and you will get a pretty good picture of what bridge assessment is about." I pass his advice and his text along to you in appendix 4.

The city of Portland needed a bridge for its trail system. Three were in contention, and Al Halbeisen was charged with figuring out which of the three bridges would best serve the city at this particular place and time. His recommendations would be based on the bridges' condition, the cost of restoring them for pedestrian use, and the cost of moving them into place over the Grand River. Appendix 4 contains Al Halbeisen's initial bridge study and budget estimate. A bridge study is a status report on your bridge, a type of inventory of good and bad things that a preservation team must consider when making restoration decisions. The Kent Street Bridge was ultimately the bridge selected for the city trail system. It is from such an initial study that a detailed budget is drafted. This next set of plans is often referred to as the engineer's estimate of probable costs.

A Structural Engineer's Assessment

Rather than being satisfied by the analysis of Portland's three bridges and the development of restoration plans for the Kent Street Bridge, my curiosity had been heightened. Perhaps yours has been also. I recalled the Marantette Bridge, with its high, gangly verticals pitted from 100 years of Michigan weather extremes, and wondered how anyone could really know if its metal was still good enough for today. I remembered the Big Hill Road Bridge, with its pack rust and buckling top plates and thought, "How does anyone actually calculate the extent of metal degradation caused by such section loss?" I remembered seeing individual parts of the Gale Road Bridge stacked alongside a county transportation garage and questioned, "Who in the world could understand the interplay of forces on a bridge that was in a pile?"

These were the questions that made my interview with Al Halbeisen seem a bit incomplete. I needed to know how an engineer quantifies the deterioration of a century-old bridge to be able to give specific recommendations about what pieces need to be repaired, replaced, or left as they are. I really wanted to know what actually goes on inside an engineer's mind when he or she is at the bridge evaluating the condition of each old, rusty part. So I turned to Frank Hatfield, professor emeritus of civil engineering at Michigan State University.

Professor Hatfield was readily available for this assignment, as he had been a member of the writing team of this book from its beginning. It was his academic insight and real-world experiences in structural engineering that had kept *A Bridge Worth Saving* from straying too far into folklore and anecdotal wit. Frank Hatfield had been the engineering compass that had kept the writing team right on track.

We met to talk at the Gale Road Bridge, which had been recently re-erected in the Calhoun County Historic Bridge Park.

"Collecting the facts is not the hard part," Frank said as we walked together on top of the newly installed wood-planked deck of this 122-foot Pratt through truss. "Most sophomore civil engineering students could do it. It simply requires a caliper and tape measure, a reference manual or two, and a methodical mind. However, interpreting the facts and drawing conclusions as to the overall safety of the bridge require advanced training and years of experience."

Frank began his demonstration by slowly walking around the bridge like a bird dog stalking a field, knowing something was there when everyone else thought the field was empty.

"I would be looking for a certain piece of metal." Frank said, continuing to walk slowly around the bridge.

"I need to find, if at all possible, a piece of metal that has not deteriorated. By measuring the dimension of this surviving piece of metal, I can evaluate the condition of other similar pieces of metal. Since most of these old bridges were rated at 100 pounds per square foot, a 10 percent loss of section would still allow the bridge to exceed AASHTO's 85-pound-per-square-foot rating for a pedestrian bridge."

He quickly qualified: "A one-to-one correlation may not always work, because compression members can suffer loss of section and still be rated at nearly 100 percent. Tension members, on the other hand, are compromised by even the smallest of gauge reductions."

"Take me through the process," I said, trying to get to a handle on what needed to be done first. I pointed to a diagonal tension member. "How do you know, for example, the strength of this particular piece of the bridge?"

"First, I need to establish an approximate age of the metal. By knowing the year that the metal was made, I can estimate its strength."

"How?" I pressed.

"AASHTO's *Manual for Condition Evaluation of Bridges* provides year-by-year approximate ratings for the strength values of steel. If I'm lucky, I might be able to identify the mill from which the metal came. In this case, I could really pin down the inherent strength of the steel."

"What would be a typical strength of steel in a bridge built around 1900?"

"Approximately 26,000 pounds per square inch.

"If I know the strength of steel," Frank continued, "and I know the dimensions of the bridge, and I know how each member relates to each other, that is, I understand the mechanics of the truss on a mathematic level, I can calculate how much stress is placed on any particular member. I then can determine if that particular member can bear its required load."

I kept pressing for an example, so we walked over to one corner of the bridge, where the inclined endpost rested on the abutment bearing plate.

"We know that a pedestrian bridge must be able to sustain an 85-pound-per-square-foot load. OK. Let's multiply the length of the bridge (122 feet) by its width (17 feet) and then multiply that square footage by 85. We should then know that the maximum capacity of the bridge must exceed approximately 88 tons (176,000 pounds)."

Frank made sure I was following his logic. He was a very patient teacher.

"We then must add," he continued, "the weight of the structure, let's say, for example, 39 tons, because the bridge must also support its own weight. In total, 127 tons of force is being exerted on all four feet [corners] of this bridge."

A formula seemed to be surfacing.

"Since all of the weight of the bridge and its potential load rest equally distributed on all four corners, I simply need to divide by four to determine the amount of force being exerted vertically at this one corner."

My eyes widened.

$$\frac{(\text{length} \times \text{width} \times 85 \text{ lbs.}) + \text{weight of bridge}}{4} = \text{vertical force on (1) corner}$$

"However," Frank continued, "since the inclined endpost is not point-ing directly down, this vertical force must be divided by the sine of its angle of inclination in order to arrive at the force being exerted specifically on the diagonal member. We must also consider how this force is being transferred throughout the truss. For every force in one direction, there is a counterforce in another."

The conversation was becoming more complex than a humanities degree could keep up with, so I deferred to his explanation with a smile. Professor Hatfield knew I had had enough trigonometry for one day.

We then talked for a brief time about pins, bolts, and rivets. "How do you know if the pins are still good?" I asked.

"They will be visually inspected and tested with a process called dye penetration. The use of dye penetration has been around for a long time. It is a process in which a low-viscosity dye is painted on the pins, and then, after it has had time to seep into the tiniest of cracks, it is wiped off the surface. A chalky white substance is then applied to the pin's surface. The remaining dye in any cracks will become magnified on the chalky surface. There is a downside to dye penetration. It can only detect cracks on the surface. Radiograph analysis, a type of X-ray for metal, can pinpoint cracks inside the metal, but the cost of a radiograph analysis is often more painful than its cure."

Frank amplified his point perfectly: "A local machine shop could fab-ricate one of these pins for approximately $150. Sending the old pins to an NDT (nondestructive testing) lab may cost twice that much."

"Isn't that the dilemma?" I said. "Why would anyone pay $300 to see if an old, rusty, pitted pin is still up to spec, if a new one could be made for half the price?"

"The engineer's job is to assess the structural worthiness of the bridge and specify which parts or sections of the bridge need to be replaced or repaired. The project team, the consultant, the preservation officer, the DOT representative, and others must clarify the team's overall commitment to historical detail."

Frank then qualified his introductory civil engineering lesson one last time. "What we have been doing up to this point is simply gathering information. The real challenge of bridge assessment comes when the engineer must deduce complex factors of safety affected not only by the physical makeup of the bridge but also by its environment and use—for example, the interplay of wind loads, concentrated loads such as truck wheels, and shifting of loads such as what occurs when a vehicle passes over the bridge."

At the beginning of the lesson, I had assumed that the assessment of a bridge was a relatively simple process for an engineer. I now understood that it is quite a complicated process, *even* for an engineer. It is more than the measuring of metal or the counting of rivets. It requires the consideration of many interactive forces and changing situations. It is seldom about what can be done but more often about what should be done. Assessment is ultimately about wisdom.

CHAPTER 6

Taking Your Bridge Apart

I f you review the previous five chapter titles, you will detect a logical and systematic process for getting ready to restore a bridge. These preliminary tasks are inescapable jobs that must be completed before any physical restoration work begins. However, just as you are about to begin the very thing you worked so diligently to prepare for, ironically, it is taken away from you. This is the time when the layperson must let go and the professional must begin.

Why, then, these final three chapters? Why bother with the nuts and bolts of metal fabrication if the contractor is going to take care of everything? These chapters are being offered to the layperson to provide a working knowledge of the actual restoration process. Your insight will encourage second opinions. Your awareness will keep everyone on his or her toes. In the preservation business, a little bit of knowledge *is* a good thing, and if you do your homework well, you just might catch the professionals whispering behind your back, "These guys really know what they're talking about."

These final chapters are being offered to the professionals for a different reason. The type of restoration work this book promotes is not a civil engineer's normal bread-and-butter work. Historic preservation work raises unique engineering challenges and often calls for creative engineering solutions. Whether it is the veteran transportation administrator or the weathered engineer, those on the preservation team need to keep their eyes open to options—some old and some never before realized. We believe you *can* teach old dogs new tricks, but the dogs must hold still long enough to see the possibilities. If the writing solicits from either the layperson or the professional "Ah, I didn't realize that was possible" or "So that's how you do it," it will have been well worthwhile.

The process of restoring a bridge is actually quite simple. One need only take the bridge apart, fix whatever is broken, get rid of the rust, repaint all the pieces, and then put everything back together. In these final chapters, we review these tasks with five bridges:

- The 133rd Avenue Bridge, a 64-foot half-hip pin-connected pony truss that spanned the Rabbit River in Hopkins Township, Allegan County, Michigan, erected by the Michigan Bridge Company, 1897.
- The 20 Mile Road Bridge, a 70-foot all-riveted Pratt pony truss that spanned the St. Joseph River in Clarendon Township, Calhoun County, Michigan, pre-1906.
- The Gale Road Bridge, a 122-foot single-span Pratt through truss, from the Grand River in Onondaga Township, Ingham County, Michigan, fabricated by the Lafayette Bridge Company of Lafayette, Indiana, 1897.
- The Charlotte Highway Bridge, a 177-foot single-span double-intersection Pratt truss (Whipple design), from the Grand River, Danby Township, Ionia County, fabricated by the Buckeye Bridge Company of Cleveland, Ohio, 1886.
- The Bauer Road Bridge, a 78-foot single-span Pratt through truss from the Looking Glass River, Watertown Township, Clinton County, Michigan, fabricated by the Penn Bridge Works of Beaver Falls, Pennsylvania, 1880.

Restoration of these bridges for the Calhoun County Historic Bridge Park has been guided by county engineer Dennis Randolph, steel fabricator Vernon Mesler. and a variety of other support personnel. Each bridge presented unusual challenges that sometimes required solutions not typically found in technical handbooks. At every stage of the restoration process, the engineers and metal fabricators tried to be faithful to historic detail. At times, even the work techniques used at the site reflected old-fashioned practices. For example, the restored Gale Road Bridge was re-erected by a team of three metal fabricators using nothing more than a gin pole and hand tools similar to what would have been available at the end of the nineteenth century. These bridges and others in the Calhoun County Historic Bridge Park will serve as a working laboratory in which to study the process of metal-truss bridge restoration.

Disassembling the Bridge

Much like a child's Erector set, late-nineteenth-century and early-twentieth-century metal-truss bridges usually arrived at the bank of the river in ready to be assembled kits. They were so self-contained and ready to be put together that it is surprising local communities could not buy them through the Sears catalogue. As the photograph suggests, one needed only a wrench and a strong back to be part of the construction team. The old metal-truss bridge

Putting together a truss bridge took some community muscle.

had been perfectly designed to be put together on-site and is consequently now quite easy to take apart.

Many contractors today are initially intimidated by the prospect of having to disassemble a bridge carefully enough so that it can be re-erected. Contractors are more used to cutting up old bridges simply to get rid of them. Usually with no experience in riveting and little experience with steel older than they are, these iron rookies may dismiss as impractical or too expensive the idea of disassembling a bridge for restoration and reassembly. Contractors who have been around for a while are more apt to say, "Sure, I can take that thing apart."

When is it wise to disassemble a bridge to restore it, as opposed to repairing it in place? Five things must be considered in answering this question: the bridge's environment, the general condition of the bridge, the local traffic needs, the size of the bridge, and the amount of money available for its restoration.

Environment

On-site repair work can affect a bridge's environment adversely. Rigorous environmental standards require contractors to use special scaffolding, protective tents, portable vacuum devices, and collection bins when working on-site to keep contaminants from the environment. The cost of complying with these standards can easily exceed the cost of removing the bridge and restoring it in a controlled, environmentally safe setting.

On-location repair work can be quite time-consuming because of the sheer difficulty of accessing all the parts of the bridge as it stands over the river. If the bridge is out in the middle of nowhere, simply getting to and from it every day can eat up a big portion of the budget. Since the hourly rate for field labor is higher than shop labor and since on-location work is without question more time-consuming, it often makes more sense to take the time to disassemble the bridge, ship it to an enclosed worksite where it can be worked on efficiently, and then re-erect it when the work has been completed.

Condition and Traffic Needs

Rust can so undermine a bridge that when it is removed, hardly any original metal is left at all. Repairs to such seriously damaged metal should not be attempted while the bridge is in place, because the load-bearing structure of the bridge is compromised in the process. If the bridge has rusted beyond light to moderate surface rust or if it is damaged more than cosmetically, it must be removed from the river before it is repaired.

It is impossible to clean a bridge thoroughly without taking it apart, because rust forms in the joints and between metal plates, making it virtually inaccessible to abrasive cleaning while assembled. This is called pack rust, and most nineteenth- and early-twentieth-century bridges have it. Although there are ways to eliminate much of this pack rust without taking the bridge apart (see chapter 7 for more information about pack rust), the only way to remove it completely is to separate the riveted seams and connections and clean each piece individually.

If a bridge is located on a main transportation corridor, the inconvenience of rerouting traffic while the bridge is disassembled for repair may make disassembly politically impractical. If such a bridge is to continue to serve traffic, a way must be found to repair it in place while traffic continues to flow.

Size and Budget

Metal-truss bridges shorter than 100 feet and lighter than 20 tons are usually easy to lift off the river and take apart. Some very small bridges can actually be snatched with a single crane, put on a flatbed truck, and hauled away to the repair facility—all in one piece. As the size of the bridge increases, so does the cost of taking it apart, eventually exceeding the disassembly cost-to-benefit threshold.

Restoration work on a bridge that has been taken apart typically lasts longer than work done in the field. The ability to remove all the rust, the chance to replace weak connections with new rivets or bolts, and the opportunity to fabricate and reinstall replacement parts in a controlled setting will definitely improve the final product. It may be more expensive up front to disassemble a bridge, but when the costs are amortized over a longer period of time, they may actually be cheaper. The bias of the writing team is clear. Whenever possible, it is best to disassemble a bridge for restoration.

A Case in Point

I first saw Nels Raynor as he was walking a wide-flange beam high over a construction site on a cold winter morning. From the ground, he appeared to be a cross between Rudolph Nureyev and Grizzly Adams. Up close, he was soft-spoken and genteel. His story was important to me, because he was the person responsible for removing the Charlotte Highway Bridge from the banks of the Grand River, and I needed to know how it was done. It was cold outside, and neither of us had much time for the interview, so we decided to sit in my car to talk and keep warm at the same time. I got right to the point. "How did you get that thing off the river?" I asked.

Almost before my words had suggested a question, he began, "We cut the modern steel deck off with a torch and removed it in pieces. We also removed the guardrails and the floor stringers. By removing the bed and all other non-load-bearing steel, we were able to reduce the overall weight of the bridge by about 15 percent." He then grabbed a legal pad from the car console and began to draw and talk at the same time. "We used two cranes, a 100-ton boom on the south side of the river, and a 275-ton hydraulic crane on the north side. Each crane was offset about 45 degrees from the ends of the bridge so we could swing the bridge away from its abutments."

I began duplicating his artwork on my notepad to confirm that I understood what he was saying.

"Before we could lift the bridge, we had to disconnect it from its abutments." His story digressed for a moment as he explained that most metal-truss bridges are anchored on one end and free-floating on bearings on the other to allow for expansion and contraction throughout the seasons. For some reason, neither side of the Charlotte Highway Bridge was anchored at that time. He continued, "We then began to lift each end of the bridge slowly."

"How were the crane lines attached? " I interrupted cautiously so as not to break the stride of his story.

"The lines were not attached directly to the bridge but to two wide-flange beams which had been threaded through the trusses under the top chord to better distribute the lifting force. We then chained these beams to the frame of the bridge so that they would not slip. When the bridge had cleared the abutments by about three feet, we slowly swung it over the river parallel to its original stand."

Cranes work to lift the Charlotte Highway Bridge off its abutments for shipment to the Calhoun County Historic Bridge Park. (See cover for the rehabilitated bridge on display at the park.)

"So the bridge was literally dangling in midair over the river?" I asked.

"Yep." He said, confirming the image I had formed in my mind.

"If it was supported by cranes on opposite sides of the river, how did you pull it to land?"

"We lowered one end of the bridge onto a barge that had been secured by cables to trees to keep it from drifting down the river. As the bridge was pulled off the river, we adjusted the length of the cables so the barge would follow the bridge to land."

"What did you use to pull it off the river?"

"A small back hoe. Since one end of it was floating on a barge and the other end was being pulled by a pole trailer, it didn't take much horsepower to bring it to land. Once the bridge had been pulled to land, we drove H-piles vertically along the side of each truss to keep the sides standing. We then removed the top struts and lateral bracing. The bridge had been bolted together at major joints. Rivets had been used almost everywhere else."

"You then lowered each side to the ground to be further disassembled, right?" I interrupted, letting him know I was not a complete novice at this sort of thing.

Another large truss, the Kent Street Bridge, being disassembled using the same techniques used for the Charlotte Highway Bridge. H-piles hold the bridge up so it can be taken apart without twisting any of the steel members.

A segment of the Kent Street Bridge on blocks on the ground, ready for transport to a shop for repair and painting.

"Not exactly." he answered. "Metal trusses are not designed to work at a 45-degree angle. If we had simply removed the H-piling and lowered the entire side down to the ground in one piece, the eyebars would have been subjected to reverse stress, and we would have run the risk of bending them. So we unbolted the sections of the top and bottom chords where they had been spliced (sometimes we had to cut the bolts with a torch) and lowered each section one at a time. Once each section was on the ground, we disassembled it in small enough pieces to place on the truck."

We were about to go our separate ways when he added an important point. "Oh, I forgot to tell you. Before we started the disassembly, we marked every piece very carefully, because we knew that eventually, someone else was going to have to put it all back together."

There had been a matter-of-fact but sincere tone to all his words, as if all this was old hat to him yet something that he really enjoyed doing.

The task of removing the 177-foot, 50-ton Charlotte Highway Bridge from the Grand River and transporting it to Marshall, Michigan, for repair took fifteen days to complete: six days to prepare the bridge for lifting, one day to lift the bridge off the river and pull it to land, and eight days to disassemble it, load it onto a flatbed truck, and haul it away. (Two trips were required.) The total cost, which included all personnel, materials, and equipment, was approximately $59,000.

Every bridge disassembly project is unique. It is unwise to assume that what worked at one location will work at all others. The contractor charged with the task should spend a good amount of time walking the bridge and carefully studying its environment in order to come up with the best approach. It is also very important to articulate the disassembly instructions in the formal contract.

In summary, consider a few general recommendations appropriate to all bridge disassembly projects:

- *Make as few cuts as possible.* Bolts and pins can be loosened with heat and the proper-size wrench. Rivets can be removed with a rivet blaster or torch. Your goal should be to preserve as much of the original metal as possible. The cutting torch should always be the last resort.
- *Use a dependable marking system.* Old bridges have a way of bending and stretching over time. What was once a perfectly symmetrical and

tight-fitting structure may today be a jigsaw-puzzle nightmare waiting to happen. Each piece of the bridge should be sensibly marked so that someone else could easily understand how to put it back together at a later date. The marks should be indelible enough to withstand transportation, outdoor storage, and time. An accompanying marking system key should be created and kept in the bridge's paperwork file. Whatever marking system you choose—metal tags or colored numbers—make sure that you use it religiously.

- *Take lots of pictures.* You will be tempted to stand 100 feet away from the bridge in order to capture the entire image in one shot. A few photos like this from various angles will be good. However, don't forget close-ups. Take lots of close-ups. Keep a journal of what you shot as you take the pictures, so that when the photos come back from the developing lab, you can label them properly. It can be quite difficult to describe the proper location of each close-up image when you get the pictures back from the lab a few days later. Shoot and develop your photographs a few days before the bridge is taken apart, lest you discover your camera did not work properly and nothing turned out.

- *Don't throw anything away.* Metal pieces that seem irrelevant may be assets in disguise. They may be used for chemical analysis or fabricated into repair parts. They can make good templates for creating replacement parts. Pieces of the old bridge also may be used in fund-raising or for generating public support. However tempted you may be to discard leftover remnants of your bridge, don't throw anything away.

The task of disassembling a bridge is a challenging endeavor and well within reach of most preservation budgets. Not all preservation projects require such a major undertaking, but going the extra mile to take a bridge apart and thoroughly repair and repaint it in an environmentally controlled setting may be the best way to go.

CHAPTER 7

Removing Rust and Painting Your Bridge

Chemically speaking, rust is iron oxide, most often found in nature as Fe_2O_3. This ubiquitous reddish-brown compound forms when two atoms of iron combine with three atoms of oxygen. Iron atoms have a tendency to give up a few of their electrons, and oxygen atoms have a tendency to want to take on a few electrons. One might say iron and oxygen are two common elements in nature that enjoy being together.

Bridges rust when their metal is exposed to air. Water and salt may nudge the process along, but the real culprit is oxygen. The battleship on the ocean floor slowly rusts away not because it is submerged in water but rather because it is exposed to oxygen dissolved in the water. The old car left in the desert will rust to oblivion despite its dry environment, because it is oxidizing. A bridge in Michigan rusts more readily than one in Arkansas because road salts used in wintertime in Michigan form a type of acid that can break down the paint that protects the metal from oxygen. Salt is also a deliquescent, a compound that naturally absorbs moisture from the air, and water, nature's universal solvent, is always happy to speed the process of oxidization along.

Whether rust is found on a swing set on a playground or a stack of steel at a scrap yard, rust is rust is rust. The bridge preservationist must deal with

Surface rust covers this beam, resulting in small pits on the metal's outside surface. Without protective paint, steel trusses suffer the ravages of rust. Also note that pack rust has pushed up the steel in between the rivets, creating a wavy look on the top plate.

Aaron T. Brodeur

three distinctive types of problems caused by rust: surface rust, pack rust, and loss of section caused by rust, sometimes complete rust-through.

Surface rust is an early indicator of paint problems and general neglect. Surface rust is the most common form of bridge rust and is the easiest to manage. The sooner you address it, the better. Ask DOT maintenance employees, and they will tell you, "You can delay repointing the cut stone abutments, you can even postpone resurfacing the deck, but never get behind in keeping your bridge rust-free."

The second and more serious type of rust a bridge preservationist will encounter is pack rust. As the name implies, this type of rust accumulates in hard-to-get-to places such as joints, seams, and riveted members. It is notorious for buckling top chord members because rust takes up more space than the iron it is made from and consequently creating pressure within a confined space, much the same way ice can buckle a watering can left out in wintertime. Pack rust ferments deep inside the structure of the bridge and is very inaccessible to cleaning.

A well-intentioned consultant may dodge the problem of pack rust by saying, "I'd sure like to be able to save this bridge, but there is just no way to get the pack rust out, unless we take everything apart and clean each piece individually." "Wrong," says Vern Mesler, and with years of experience in restoring metal-truss bridges at the Calhoun County Historic Bridge Park, he knows something about rust. Vern Mesler and his crew developed an effective solution for some forms of pack rust:

> One day, my restoration crew pointed out to me that as they drove a new rivet near a buckle, the rust broke up and was driven from the buckle. This gave me an idea for not only flattening the plates, but also for removing the rust (called pack rust) that forms inside.
>
> Using a rivet gun, we hammered a buckle, and the rust inside the buckle broke up and was driven from the buckle. However, the hammering left scarring on the exterior metal, and I was also concerned about work hardening the plate. To avoid scarring and to get more impact from the

Tackling pack rust removal led to making some new tools. First, Vern Mesler modified an old rivet gun by blunting the end (right side). Then he made a small steel plate with a handle to protect the bridge metal from the hammering of the rivet gun (left side).

Aaron T. Brodeur

Aaron T. Brodeur

ABOVE: Heating the bridge metal over the pack rust is the first step in removing it.

LEFT: Workers use the rivet gun to pound on the pack rust, turning it to dust and removing most of it.

Using the heat and rivet gun also straightens the steel, reducing the buckling. The left side shows the repaired area, and the right side still contains pack rust.

hammering of the rivet gun, I had the crew take an old snap from a rivet gun and blunt the end.

We still had some scarring, and I was still concerned with work hardening the plate. We continued experimenting with the amount of heat on the buckles. I decided to keep it to approximately 750 degrees F, well below the 1,200-degree transformation range of steel, to avoid any problems in creating hard or brittle areas. To further reduce scarring, we fabricated a steel plate with a handle to serve as a buffer between the hammering of the rivet gun and the buckle.

We began sequencing the heating to prevent distortion; that is, we removed a few buckles in one area and then moved on to other buckles further away to keep from concentrating too much heat in any one area. Taken together, these steps not only successfully removed the pack rust from between the sections of the chord members, they also eliminated the appearance of it.

Michigan Department of Transportation

Eventually, rust converts solid metal to dust, resulting in rust-through. If much of the bridge suffers from rust-through, there is little historic material to save.

Vern is the first to admit that this approach does not remove all the rust. It does, though, give the preservationist an alternative to giving up on the bridge altogether when the bridge cannot be taken apart to be cleaned.

Loss of section caused by rust is a more serious problem than surface or pack rust. Loss of section is the reduction of the cross section of any area metal from its original thickness. Notice how the in the above photo that the bottom plate has been reduced by rust. Section loss can be repaired. (See chapter 8 for information on repairing section loss.) Sometimes the loss of section is so extensive that it makes more sense simply to replace the entire member.

Theoretically, rust can be painted over, but it is unwise to do so. Paint requires a stable surface to bond to, and rust is anything but stable. As the rust flecks off, so will the paint. Painting over rust can produce a momentary sigh of relief for the maintenance employee, but it is ultimately a waste of time and money.

In the case of Vern's pack rust solution, paint was applied not to rust but rather to the cleaned surfaces that surrounded it, isolating the remaining rust from the elements. As long as the protective coating is secure and the rusty area is deprived of oxygen, painting rust in can stop its progression. This is precisely what Vern's restoration crew did when they shattered the rust loose, hammered and heated the top plate into alignment, cleaned the exposed surfaces, and then repainted everything.

"Just how clean does clean need to be?" is more of a practical question than a theoretical one. Project standards for your bridge will be established through a collaboration among the consultant-engineer, the project manager (if different from the engineer), and usually a state preservation official and a representative from the department of transportation. The bridge's environment and its ultimate use will be taken into consideration in determining the paint system for your bridge, which in turn will determine the level of cleaning needed for your bridge.

Say "abrasive cleaning," and almost everyone thinks "sand-blasting." Sand, however, is seldom used today. Professionals have discovered many media alternatives that clean better than sand and are more environmentally friendly.

Professional blasters rely on three types of abrasive media: natural, such as sand, flint, or industrial garnet; by-product, such as mineral slag, nutshells, or corn cobs; and manufactured, such as glass beads, plastic grit, steel shot, or even Styrofoam. Choosing the right media for blasting is like traversing a bridge on its top chord while juggling a handful of hot rivets—you really need to pay attention to what you're doing. The professional blaster can make the trip successfully by asking the right questions:

- Will the work be performed on-site or at a commercial shop?
- What type of metal is your bridge made of?
- What is the condition of the metal? Just how rusty is it?
- What type of paint needs to be removed? Is it toxic? Does it need to be separated from the media before disposal?
- Is the bridge located on a remote country road or near a residential neighborhood? Will it be closed to traffic during cleaning, or will traffic continue to use it during cleaning?
- What type of paint will be reapplied? What type of anchor pattern does the paint call for?

After reviewing the project plans and the paint specifications established by the project team, the blasting professional will be able to recommend a medium best suited for the job.

Most state departments of transportation have formal protocols for painting bridges. Trust their recommendations. Bridges along the New England coastline, which must endure cold winters exposed to salty air, require a different painting system from bridges in the hot, dry climate of Arizona. Of the five regions listed below, all recommend a three-coat system. Maine uses a moisture-cure urethane system, which allows paint to be applied throughout the winter. Oregon, one of the most constantly humid areas of the country, uses a micaceous iron oxide paint which, because of its mica-based molecular structure, is extremely resistant to moisture. All regions use some form of zinc primer as the base coat, because zinc bonds well with steel.

Paint Protocols

- *Maine.* coat 1: Zinc primer
  coat 2: Mio-mastic
  coat 3: Aliphatic urethane
- *S. Carolina (inland).* coat 1: Inorganic zinc primer
  coat 2: Acrylic
  coat 3: Acrylic
- *S. Carolina (coastal).* coat 1: Inorganic zinc primer
  coat 2: Aluminum epoxy mastic
  coat 3: Aliphatic urethane
- *Michigan.* coat 1: Corothane zinc primer
  coat 2: Corothane mastic
  coat 3: Corothane aliphatic finish
- *Oregon.* coat 1: Zinc filled urethane
  coat 2: Micaceous iron oxide filled
  coat 3: Moisture-cured polyurethane

Cleaning and painting your bridge can become the largest expense of your preservation budget. The cost will be based on its type, location, size, condition, the kind of paint that must be removed, and the paint that will be applied. To determine a reliable cost estimate, your bridge must be assessed carefully by an experienced cleaning and painting firm.

If old lead paint must be removed, the cost of cleaning can significantly exceed the cost of painting. Special precautions must be taken to remove the hazardous material, and significantly more money must be paid to dispose of it properly.

In certain climates, with certain types of metal, and under certain conditions of use, a metal bridge may be left unpainted. Like the iron sculpture that reddens naturally with the passing of time, an old bridge may do quite well without complying to a rigorous three-coat paint standard. Wrought iron by its very chemical makeup is quite rust-resistant. Bridge steel before the 1920s had a high phosphorus content, which likewise made it much more rust-resistant than modern-day steel. Critical joints may be strategically painted with a color to match the rest of the rusting span, or one protective coat over everything may be all the bridge really needs. If your budget is tight and the circumstances warrant, consider letting your bridge grow old rust-fully.

CHAPTER 8

Repairing Damaged Bridge Parts

U nlike wooden bridges that rot and burn or concrete bridges that eventually slip beyond the point of no-patch return, metal-truss bridges can almost always be repaired. By their very nature, they are fixable. Bent metal can be straightened. Rust-through can be welded shut. Broken pieces can be made whole again. This chapter is about fixing broken bridges. It is about flame-straightening, welding, riveting, and the age-old question that haunts every preservationist: "Should we repair this old piece of metal, or should we replace it with new steel?"

Flame-Straightening

I was sure you had to stretch it, bang it, pound it, and ratchet it back into place with the same type of vigorous force that had caused it to bend in the first place. I had no idea that the best way to straighten a bent piece of steel was simply to heat it up. Flame-straightening has been a metal fabricator's secret weapon for decades, and today it is still the best technique for bringing bent metal back into line.

A bent beam before heat straightening.

Aaron T. Brodeur

I first witnessed the art of flame-straightening at the Calhoun County transportation garage in Marshall, Michigan. A small group of MDOT employees had come down from Lansing for a historic bridge restoration seminar. When I arrived, the group was already huddling around master metal fabricator Vern Mesler. Decked in typical welding garb, with a heating torch in his right hand and a piece of chalk in his left, Vern hovered over an eight-foot-long wide-flange beam, ready to teach.

"What I want to show you today is called flame-straightening." Vern said as he lit his heating torch and adjusted it to a tight blue flame that looked and sounded like the exhaust of a miniature jet engine.

"By applying just the right amount of heat at just the right place, I will be able to make this bent flange pull itself back into line."

Vern's words were greeted with interest and skepticism.

He took the chalk as if to sketch an assignment to his class, but rather

Using a heating torch, a Calhoun County Historic Bridge Park worker flame-straightens the bridge beam.

Aaron T. Brodeur

than writing on a slate, he drew on steel—two quick hash marks in the shape of a V and two more in the same direction a few inches away.

"I've determined the points where the metal needs to contract in order to pull the surrounding segments into line," Vern explained. He then began to move the torch back and forth on the steel within the triangular areas he had drawn.

I was a bit more prepared for this demonstration than the others, because Vern had given me a box full of reading material to digest beforehand. A 1955 article from *Welding Engineer,* by Joseph Holt, had already alerted me to flame-straightening:

> Use of the oxyacetylene flame in performing difficult—even seemingly impossible—tasks in steel work is often underestimated. There are many jobs that beginners as well as old-timers pass by because they are not acquainted

with the advantages offered by contractive forces which set in after heat has been properly applied.

The "contraction method" will always help in straightening bent steel members, or in bending steel members for fabrication. The author has used this method to straighten . . . steel bridge portals, batter posts, wind-braces and chords without removing them from their original positions. Other bridge parts also have been repaired in place with no traffic hold-up. . . . The process is applicable to all steel shapes. So far, however, it has received little attention from the average welder—a man who should find it of great value in everyday work.

—Joseph Holt, *Welding Engineer* 40, no. 10 (October 1955)

When steel is heated, it expands in volume, not in line. Instead of forcing the surrounding material (which acts almost like a vise) to move, the heated steel expands into itself. Metal fabricators call this "upsetting." However, steel that cools has great "pulling strength." This causes the contracting metal to pull the surrounding metal into a new shape determined by the pattern of contraction the heat has caused.

When we speak of heat "pulling" the steel, we must remember that properly applied heat only forces the metal to "upset" (or expand into itself), and that contraction as the metal cools is the force which pulls it towards the desired point.

—Joseph Holt, *Welding Engineer* 40, no. 10 (October 1955)

It seems that heated steel does not push very well, but cooling steel is very good at pulling. I was beginning to understand. The "V" patterns Vern made on the steel now made sense to me. He placed them strategically to pull the steel back into line.

"Does the heating and cooling of the steel damage it in any way?" I asked Vern as he continued to work on the bent flange.

"Not if you keep the temperature below its transformation threshold, which is approximately 1,200 degrees Fahrenheit for the type of steel we are using today," he replied.

"How do you know what the temperature is at any given moment?" I quickly followed up.

"I usually can tell by the color of the steel. If I need to be exact, I use heat sticks, crayon-like markers that are designed to melt at various temperatures."

"How long does it take to bend a flange, let's say, two inches?"

"Each heating and cooling of the metal will bend the piece a slight degree. Usually, the process has to be repeated several times to achieve the desired correction."

Like watching the minute hand of a clock, I stared at the contracting steel, believing I could see the metal moving ever so slightly. It was not until the process had been repeated several times and Vern had placed a string against the flange to compare the new configuration with its original deformity that we all could see the significant realignment caused by the contracting forces of the cooling steel.

Flame-straightening is more than a metal fabricator's trick of the trade. It is a proven technique, which in the hands of an experienced metal fabricator can bring most any bent piece of metal back into line. Just ask Vern and his MDOT students. Flame-straightening really works.

Welding

I stood on the Gale Road Bridge with Vern and two of his assistants as they were installing a restored vertical. I asked, "Is this vertical original?" "Part of it is," Vern replied as he pointed to where he had joined a new channel section onto the original piece with a full-penetration weld. As much as I tried, I could not see the weld. It had been ground out with such care that it seemed to vanish into the natural grain of the metal.

"Is it just as strong as the original?" I asked more seriously.

"Yes." Vern replied.

On another occasion, Vern and I stood on top of a heap of bridge parts outside the Calhoun County Road Commission garage.

"What are you going to do with those disintegrated eyebar heads?" I asked.

"I'm planning to repair them." Vern said.

"No way." I gasped.

"I can fix them with a technique called padding," he explained.

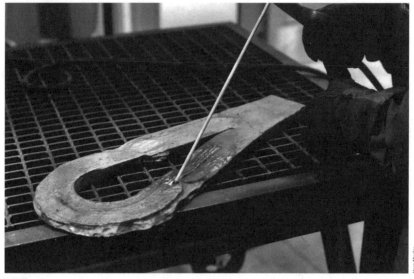

Loss of section refers to a loss in the thickness of a metal beam or other bridge part such as an eyebar from rust. Often, these parts are thrown away, but they can be repaired with a process called padding. Here, padding helps build up the metal in an eyebar so it can be reused.

The top part of the eyebar shows loss of section, while the bottom shows the results of padding where metal has been restored to its desired thickness.

"You've got to be kidding." I insisted. To a layperson, the disintegration of the steel seemed beyond repair. Vern assured me it could be fixed with padding.

Padding, a welding technique to repair section loss on bridge parts, builds up the damaged metal by fusing new metal onto the old. After new metal has been applied and left to cool, excess material is ground away to match the proper dimension and surface pattern of the original steel.

Look closely at the two photos of rusted and broken eyebars that were repaired by padding.

Again, I asked, "Does this type of welding make the piece as strong as the original?"

Again, Vern replied, "Yes."

Century-old bridges can present peculiar challenges to the modern-day welder, because the composition of the metal is different from the composition of steel made today. Old steel and wrought iron are typically high in phosphorus and sulfur, which can complicate the welding process:

> [P]hosphorus is an impurity, and should be kept as low as possible. Over 0.04% makes welds brittle and increases the tendency to crack. Phosphorus also lowers the surface tension of the molten weld metal making it difficult to control. . . . Sulfur in any appreciable amount promotes hot shortness in welding, and the tendency increases with increased sulfur. It can be tolerated up to about 0.035% (with sufficient Mn), over 0.05% it can cause serious problems. Sulfur is also detrimental to surface quality in low carbon and low manganese steels.
>
> —*The Procedure Handbook of Arc Welding, Design and Practice,*
> published by Lincoln Electric Company, 1933

Vern consulted the book *Metals and How to Weld Them,* by T. B. Jefferson, and heeded its advice. By using low welding currents and fast travel speeds for welding steel with high phosphorus and by using low-hydrogen electrodes on steels with high sulfur, Vern was able to save all of the eyebars of the 133rd Avenue Bridge.

Riveting

I watched two *young* men, Wayne Conklin and Rob Denniston, demonstrating the *lost* art of riveting to a small crowd at the Calhoun County Bridge Park. I highlight the words *young* and *lost* because if the art of riveting has really been lost, it certainly is being rediscovered by a new generation of metal fabricators in Michigan. Wayne and Rob are wizards at it. They have been working at the Calhoun County Road Commission garage for the last few years under the tutelage of Vern Mesler, doing the day-to-day bridge restoration work for the Historic Bridge Park.

The crowd that Wayne and Rob were entertaining that Saturday afternoon at the Living History demonstration was not your typical welding class. It included a couple of guys who would not have missed the show any more than they would have declined to look under the hood of a car with a souped-up engine, a family of four who had been drawn to the action from their picnic blanket thirty yards away, a few other bystanders, myself, and one dog.

Although the general technique of riveting has been around for centuries, it was first used on structural iron in England in the early 1800s. For the first few decades, most riveting was done in manufacturing shops with large power tools. Eventually, portable tools were invented that allowed workers to rivet in the field. One such device, introduced in 1883, was the Boyer pneumatic hammer:

> The basic Boyer hammer has had a remarkable longevity as a tool. Ironworkers still use them . . . and the Chicago Pneumatic Tool Company continues to sell them. . . . The Boyer name was dropped from the 1991 catalog, but a hammer with an 11-inch stroke was listed that looked amazingly like a turn-of-the-century model.
>
> —David A. Simmons, "'The Continuous Clatter': Practical Field Riveting," *IA: The Journal of the Society for Industrial Archeology* 23, no. 2 (1997)

While Wayne extracted the heated rivets from a small forge next to the demonstration steel beam, Rob picked up his Boyer pneumatic·hammer to begin riveting. Wayne inserted the rivet into the hole and then grabbed a simple but important tool called the bucking bar. Both men took an attacklike

The rivet crew performing a Living History demonstration at the Calhoun County Historic Bridge Park. The man on the left uses a pneumatic (air-driven) hammer to form the rivet head, while the man on the right uses a bucking bar (not shown) to hold a preformed head in place while the hammer works its magic.

stance, and *boom!* The machine-gun-sounding Boyer began. The work seemed to vibrate their entire bodies. The sound was intense. After about twenty seconds, if that much, the men put down their tools and invited the small crowd to come closer and inspect their work.

I sneaked in a question: "How many rivets can you do in an hour?"

"About twenty," Rob answered.

Wayne clarified, "If we had one more guy to set the rivets in place and keep the rivets coming, we could double that."

Early rivet gangs, as the teams were commonly called, were typically made up of four workers. One man worked at a small forge, usually on ground level, to heat the rivets to the right temperature. He then tossed each rivet to another member of the gang, who caught it in a can. With specially design tongs, the catcher positioned the rivet in a predrilled hole. Once it was inserted, the bucker pressed the already-formed head of the rivet with a tool called the bucking bar. The driver formed the head on the other side of the rivet, either by hand with a die and a sledge hammer or with the Boyer gun, a portable pneumatic hammer.

> The rivets were bucked with various tools called goosenecks, dollys, horsecocks, spring bars, banjos, air jambs and sometimes with another rivet gun, called double gunning.
>
> —Melvin Weibe, "The Rivet Gang," *The Anvil's Ring* (Fall 1994)

"Why so many types of bucking tools?" I asked Rob.

"It all depends on where the rivet is located in the steel structure. If you need to buck a rivet in a wide flange, you're going to need to use what we call a gooseneck bucking bar in order to get to it."

It was fun watching the guys work that day and fun, too, seeing the children jump at the blast of the hammer and put their hands over their ears, with Mom and Dad trying to explain in between bursts, "That's how bridges were made a long time ago." Needless to say, the dog didn't stay too long after the first round of hammering.

Riveting may be a forgotten art, but it is not a completely lost one. Engineers may be resistant to riveting. Contractors may be unaware of its viability. Even some pretty good consultants may be under the impression that it is just too expensive. However, you must know:

- Almost every size of rivet used 100 years ago is available today by the ton. The Jay-Cee Rivets and Company of Farmington, Michigan, has a warehouse full of them. The Champion Rivet company of Cleveland, Ohio, can also help. An Internet search engine under the word *riveting* will reveal still others.
- Portable riveting equipment can still be purchased, rented, or borrowed. The Michigan Pneumatic Company of Detroit is a good first try, or consider the Chicago Pneumatic Tool Company, of Chicago, or turn again to the Internet for other sources.
- A properly riveted bridge is comparable in strength to one that has been bolted or welded.

Your preservation team may balk at the thought of re-riveting your entire bridge. But before you throw the rivets out with the river water, collaborate with people who have experience in flame-straightening. Talk with welders who understand how to work with century-old steel. Seek out craftsmen, young and old alike, who know how to rivet. Or come to the Calhoun County Bridge Park to learn for yourself. If you can handle a tool, you can learn how to rivet. The question should not be "Can we be true to the historical integrity of our bridge?" but rather "Why not?"

CHAPTER 9

Putting Your Bridge Back Together Again

"Lift it up a little more."

"OK, push."

"How's that?"

"Almost . . ."

"Oops, too much. Back up a little."

I listened carefully to the exchange of highly technical words among Wayne, Rob, and Vern as they finessed a 250-pound horizontal eyebar onto the pins of the bottom chord of the Gale Road Bridge. Wayne slowly lowered one end of the heavy piece of metal into place with the gin pole, while Rob finagled (another technical word) the vertical to which the other end had already been attached.

"Just a little bit more," said Vern as he continued to orchestrate the process verbally. A couple more whacks with a four-by-four oak beam, and the sixteenth-inch tolerance between the hole in the eyebar and the pin onto which it needed to slide surrendered to a unique combination of sweet talk and brute force.

I had the pleasure that morning of watching three grown-up men working like kids playing with a new box of Tinker Toys. I also had the rare

Vern Mesler

The Gale Road Bridge gets put back together in the Calhoun County Historic Bridge Park. The tall light-colored pole is a gin pole, used to lift heavy beams high off the ground.

opportunity of witnessing a restored metal-truss bridge being put together by hand, one piece at a time.

The creators of the Calhoun County Historic Bridge Park had always intended for the park to be more than a tourist attraction. From its conception, it was meant to be a working laboratory in which metal-truss bridge restoration techniques would be tested and evaluated. The story you are about to read was one experiment in this living laboratory of steel that sought to explore the construction methods of craftsmen who worked 100 years ago.

Vern explained, "We wanted to try to re-erect the bridge using nothing more than the same basic tools that were available in 1897 when the bridge was first put up." The caretakers of the park saw it as an opportunity to learn something. Vern saw it as a personal challenge. "I wanted to see if it could be done."

In the course of writing this book, I have had the good fortune of meeting engineers, project planners, and academicians who were all honorably dedicated to historic preservation. None of these individuals, however, embodied the spirit of metal-truss bridge preservation quite like Vern Mesler. His skill, honed by a lifetime of metal fabrication in industry and the classroom, was nothing less than astonishing. I have watched him wield a rivet gun as if it were a sculptor's chisel and have seen him command a cutting torch as if it were a calligraphy pen. His knowledge of metal fabrication is further complemented by a pure and passionate respect for honoring the craftsmanship of the original creators. To him, the metal of an old bridge is a first source document that must be carefully preserved.

The challenge before Vern on this occasion was to reconstruct the Gale Road Bridge using only the common tools that would have been available in the late nineteenth century—a gin pole, scaffolding, a couple of hand-cranked come-alongs, some pry bars, and a variety of wrenches the size of an adult human leg. Except for the gas-powered forklift, which was rented at the beginning of the project to pull the floor beams and stringers into place, and the electric motor powering the winch on the bottom of the gin pole, this 122-foot, 40-ton Pratt truss was going to be put up the old-fashioned way—by hand.

"Aren't you fudging a little bit" I said to Vern.

"What do you mean, fudging?" he replied.

"You're using an electric motor on the winch, aren't you?"

"I want to relive history, not join it."

Vern's humor quickly put the tool list into perspective and quite nicely qualified the historical purity of the project. So what if they fudged a little bit?

As I tried to keep my balance on the open stringers of the bridge's deck, Vern went to his truck and pulled out a photograph of an early-twentieth-century bridge construction site. "See there," he said, pointing to the lower right-hand corner of the picture. "They had this contraption called a gin pole." Before the advent of power tools, gin poles were commonly used for heavy lifting at small construction sites. Vern knew that if you were going to build a bridge without a crane, you had to have a gin pole.

Vern went on to tell me more about fabricating his 27-foot-tall gin pole, which weighed about 400 pounds and could lift one ton. "Pretty good lifting ratio, don't you think?" he pointed out. He also gave me a quick demonstration of the quad pod, a tool he had made to shuffle heavy pieces of metal along the stringers. Eventually, though, the bridge work tugged at him more than my questions did, so I stood back and watched quietly while he and his two assistants continued to work.

I stopped by the bridge several times over the next few months to see how the gang was doing. Vern talked to me about how he frequently had to re-level the cribbing that supported the floor beams, because the weight of the growing structure kept pushing the cribbing deeper into the mud. He also told me that he had strung piano wire from abutment to abutment to level the floor beams. I thought he was pulling my leg. "Really?" I said. "Yep, we eyeballed those floor beams level with just piano wire." On another occasion, I caught the team lifting a half-ton top chord section into place only to get it to the top of the truss and find out it was on the wrong side of the vertical. The beam had to be lowered, the equipment moved and reset, and the entire task repeated. I'll leave the group commentary that followed to your imagination. I will never forget the day the first inclined endpost went up. The sense of accomplishment was climactic. All it was, was an inclined endpost. You would have thought someone had won the lottery.

Slowly, very slowly, the 100-plus pieces of the bridge came together. Its looming profile could now be seen from the interstate highway, and more and more people were coming to the park to see what was going on. My inquiry now shifted from an interest in construction details to a more reflective understanding of the project. I now looked for answers to questions such as "What have you learned by doing this with nineteenth-century tools?" "If you had to do it over again, what would you do differently?" "What would you recommend to others contemplating such a task?" On a warm spring day, I stopped by the bridge one last time to talk to Vern.

"It is extremely slow, extremely labor-intensive work," he said while shaking his head and repeating the word *extremely* several more times. From start to finish, the re-erection of the Gale Road Bridge took six months.

I wondered, "If you had a couple of cranes and a team of five experienced iron workers, how long would it take?"

"About ten days," he replied.

"Why the big difference?"

"The problem is not connecting the pieces together, it's getting everything into position to do the work." He was referring to the gin pole and the scaffolding and other smaller but equally necessary tools for the job. "Make your tools as portable as possible," he explained. "Most of your construction time will be consumed by setting things up."

Vern then said something surprising, but the more I thought about it, the more it made sense: "Before you make any hard-fast connections, before you tighten bolts on any one panel, or anchor endplates permanently in the abutments, get the entire bridge together."

Bridges need room to move during reassembly. When you shift one element to accommodate another, all the pieces will be affected. When you pull one diagonal in line, beware that another diagonal may move out of line, ever so slightly. (Remember the sixteenth of an inch clearance of the eyebar Wayne, Rob, and Vern had to coax into place?) Therefore, the entire assembly should be kept as loose as possible in order for all the pieces ultimately to conform to the original structure. The expression Vern used was "You need to plan for wiggle room."

"Did you encounter any peculiar or unexpected challenges with this project?"

"The biggest technical challenge was putting together a skewed bridge."

"What do you mean?" I asked.

"We chose a relatively rare design that plagued almost every step of the construction. One side of the bridge was thirteen degrees askew from the other side. This meant that the abutments, the floor beams, and the lateral bracing on both the lower and upper chords had to accommodate this thirteen-degree skew."

I then asked the $10,000 question: "If you had it to do all over again, what would you do differently?" Before Vern spoke, I could see he had several answers.

"As much as we marked the bridge before it was taken down, we didn't mark it enough. If I were doing this over again, I would definitely be more thorough with the marking system. I would also keep a detailed journal of how the bridge was taken apart and would take even more photos than we did. Despite the marking system we used, which was pretty good, we periodically found ourselves asking, 'Which way does this go?'

"I would also install a temporary deck on the bridge," he added. "We left it off this time, because we were afraid of damaging the wood during the construction of the truss. Not having a deck, though, slowed us down a lot, because we were always having to move things on the open stringers. Next time, I would either put a temporary rough deck on, or I would install the final deck upside down and then turn it right-side up when the project was finished."

It was precisely this type of down-to-earth, practical thinking that made the re-erection of the Gale Road Bridge a huge success. Whether it was using a gin pole to lift heavy members or stretching piano wire to keep the bridge true, the re-erection of the Gale Road Bridge was a demonstration of old-fashioned ingenuity and modern-day common sense.

On June 29, 2002, the Gale Road Bridge was formally dedicated at the Calhoun County Historic Bridge Park. On hand were local officials, county road commissioners and employees, representatives from MDOT, the press, volunteers, and local citizens who still had a hard time believing something like this was actually happening in their town. Everyone was excited. No one, however, was prouder of the moment than Vern and his crew.

Conclusion

ecause of its river-rich topography, "over the river and through the woods" was more than a phrase in a song for the young state of Michigan. It was a way of life, and just at the time early Michiganders needed to cross the river, iron bridges were a hot item. This is why numerous Warrens, Pratts, and a few Whipples still dot the Michigan countryside today. A 1985 inventory of bridges in Michigan identified 373 metal-truss bridges still standing in the state (see table 4). Of the 167 that remain today, 10 percent are in good condition. A few more are holding their own, and as one might suspect, most of the rest need immediate attention and care.

Unlike some state DOTs that fear metal-truss bridges like the plague, Michigan's transportation leaders are becoming more and more metal-truss-friendly. In the past seventeen years, Michigan has funded twenty-five historic truss preservation projects totaling $8.5 million. A few courageous souls have stood up for Michigan's metal-truss bridges and have begun to effect real change in the way Michigan does its bridge business.

"I had this idea," said Dennis Randolph. "Some called it naive, but I thought, 'Once a good bridge, always a good bridge.' So I set out to rehabilitate the old bridges in our county to use as they were originally intended or in some other creative way."

Table 4. Metal Truss Bridge Losses from 1985–2002

BRIDGE TYPE	NUMBER ASSESSED IN 1985	NUMBER REMAINING SINCE 1985	NUMBER REPLACED SINCE 1985
Pony truss	212	77 (36%)	135 (64%)
Through truss	93	45 (48%)	48 (52%)
Steel arch	8	3 (38%)	5 (62%)
Deck truss	3	1 (33%)	2 (67%)
Misc. styles	57	41 (72%)	16 (28%)
	373	167 (45%)	206 (55%)

Dennis Randolph has worked all of his adult life as a public servant in the transportation field, first as a civil engineer, and also as the managing director of the Calhoun County Road Commission. His looks are deceiving. Underneath this mild-mannered, soft-spoken professional bureaucrat lies a nuclear engine of ideas and a relentless champion of the metal-truss bridge. We often assume that it is the flamboyant, fast-talking marketing wizard who ultimately prevails. It is just the opposite. It is the cheerful, thoughtful, pedantic public servant who really gets things done. The little red steam engine said, "I think I can, I think I can, I think I can . . ." Dennis Randolph says, "Heck, let's do it."

The *it* that Dennis Randolph is talking about is the Calhoun County Historic Bridge Park. It was a dream initially sparked by a practical dilemma: "What do we do with this old bridge?" It later blossomed into a crusade. The park is an unprecedented preservation phenomenon that not only collects old bridges but also promotes their preservation by actually showing people how to rivet, flame-straighten, and bring old, bent, rusty metal back to life. In its short five-year history, the park has done the following:

- Demystified truss bridge repair by providing a laboratory for developing practical preservation techniques.
- Assisted several communities in bridge preservation projects by offering knowledge of preservation options and ideals.
- Encouraged Michigan engineers to reexamine and value the preservation of original materials as first source documents.

- Provided hands-on bridge restoration training for metal fabrication professionals.
- Offered college and university students intern field experience in metal-truss repair.
- Offered formal apprenticeships to several young metal fabricators in the art and science of historic metal-truss bridge preservation.
- Inspired MDOT officials to adopt a new and formalized approach for working on state metal-truss bridge restoration projects.
- Uncovered unwritten history of metal-truss bridge fabrication through experimentation and research.
- Raised public awareness of metal-truss preservation through numerous newspaper and TV stories, and inspired the writing of this book.

"The strategy of my team was simple," said Dennis Randolph. "We wanted to create a workshoplike environment where our staff and consultants could experiment with the practical issues of metal-truss bridge preservation with the hopes of sharing our findings with others." The park has become a working laboratory to which transportation officials, engineers, consultants, and bridge enthusiasts from all over the country turn for inspiration and practical advice.

After two years of pursuing this story in coffee shops and conference rooms, on bridge decks in parks, small towns, and out in the middle of nowhere, we now return to the very bridge that began our story, the century-old Pratt truss over the St. Joseph River in Mendon, Michigan, called Marantette. When it closed to traffic in 1982, the Marantette Bridge went into a type of bridge limbo. Like an old car resisting the crusher, it was trying to hold on long enough to become a vintage antique. Thanks to a lady who could see the bridge every day from her kitchen window and thanks to some of her village friends who could remember playing on the bridge as children, the Marantette bridge was able to hold on long enough.

What is transpiring at the Marantette Bridge is both provincial and provocative—provincial because it is happening in the little village of Mendon, Michigan, provocative because if it can happen there, it can happen anywhere. The town folks are making phone calls, talking to neighbors, and inviting transportation and preservation officials to see their bridge. They are also beginning to raise funds to hire a consultant and complete a formal study of the bridge. They still have a long way to go, but the community seems to be on the right track. At least according to some folks down at the Blue Bird Café on Main Street, "Ain't nobody gonna want to tear that thing down now."

There is something so three-dimensionally captivating about old metal-truss bridges. Maybe it is the audacious simplicity of their design or the unpredictable patterns of their patina. Maybe it is really our subconscious pleading with us to reject the efficiency of a 55-mile-an-hour concrete slab in favor of a slow, ornate ride. Whatever it is, one thing is certain. The metal-truss bridges of Michigan, and all the many others scattered throughout our country, need our help. Not all of them can or should be saved. But some are sure worth the try.

Bridge Types and Designs

E arly iron and steel bridges relied on three basic truss designs: the through truss, the pony truss, and the deck truss. The through truss, with deck, sides, and top, tunneled vehicles through a box of interconnecting vertical, diagonal, and horizontal bracing. Most long-span metal-truss bridges were built on the through truss design. The pony truss, similar to the through truss but without a top, carried traffic on a bed attached to two side trusses. It was called a pony truss because the roadway straddled or rode in between the two parallel trusses, somewhat like the saddle on a horse. For short spans, this truss was preferred to the through truss, because it was less expensive to build. The deck truss carried the deck of the bridge on the top chord of the truss. Its supporting truss structure was below the roadway. The advantage of the deck truss is that it could accommodate vehicles of unlimited height. However, it was only used at gorgelike crossings, because it needed significant clearance below the roadway.

Truss Types

Metal bridge truss types were as varied as they were many, their names derived either from their appearance, their owners, or their inventors. The

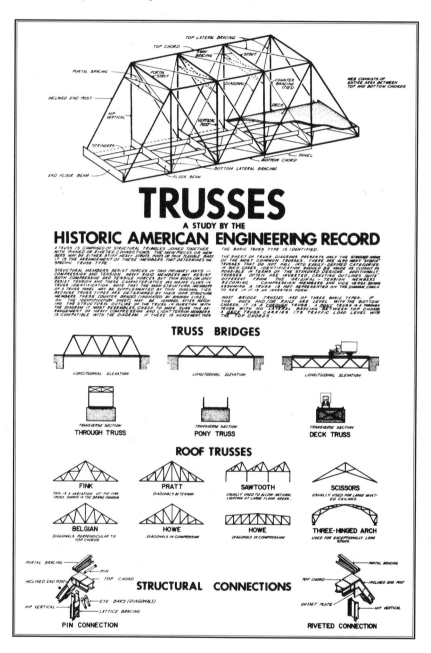

The Historic American Engineering Record collects detailed information on metal truss bridges. This illustration shows how truss designs vary.

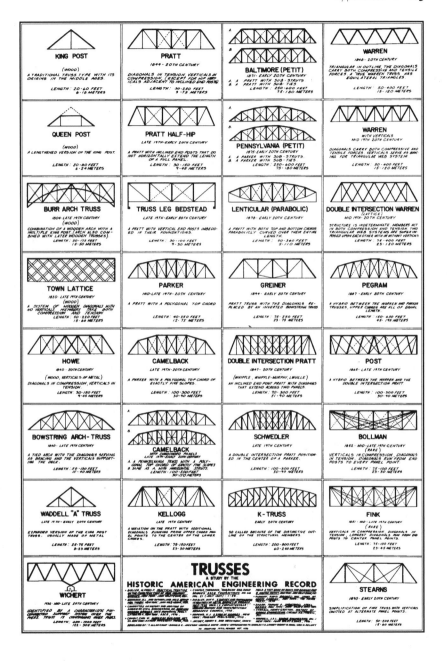

KING POST

(WOOD)
A TRADITIONAL TRUSS TYPE WITH ITS
ORIGINS IN THE MIDDLE AGES.

LENGTH: 20-60 FEET
6-18 METERS

PRATT

1844 - 20TH CENTURY
DIAGONALS IN TENSION, VERTICALS IN
COMPRESSION, (EXCEPT FOR HIP VERT-
ICALS ADJACENT TO INCLINED END POSTS)
LENGTH: 30-250 FEET
9-75 METERS

BALTIMORE (PETIT)

1871- EARLY 20TH CENTURY
A. A PRATT WITH SUB-STRUTS
B. A PRATT WITH SUB-TIES
LENGTH: 250-600 FEET
75-180 METERS

WARREN

1848 - 20TH CENTURY
TRIANGULAR IN OUTLINE THE DIAGONALS
CARRY BOTH COMPRESSIVE AND TENSILE
FORCES. A TRUE WARREN TRUSS HAS
EQUILATERAL TRIANGLES.
LENGTH: 50-400 FEET
15-120 METERS

QUEEN POST

(WOOD)
A LENGTHENED VERSION OF THE KING POST.

LENGTH: 20-80 FEET
6-24 METERS

PRATT HALF-HIP

LATE 19TH-EARLY 20TH CENTURY
A PRATT WITH INCLINED END POSTS THAT DO
NOT HORIZONTALLY EXTEND THE LENGTH
OF A FULL PANEL.
LENGTH: 30-150 FEET
9-45 METERS

PENNSYLVANIA (PETIT)

1875- EARLY 20TH CENTURY
A. A PARKER WITH SUB-STRUTS
B. A PARKER WITH SUB-TIES
LENGTH: 250-600 FEET
75-180 METERS

WARREN

WITH VERTICALS
MID 19TH-20TH CENTURY
DIAGONALS CARRY BOTH COMPRESSIVE AND
TENSILE FORCES. VERTICALS SERVE AS BRAC-
ING FOR TRIANGULAR WEB SYSTEM
LENGTH: 50-400 FEET
15-120 METERS

BURR ARCH TRUSS

1804- LATE 19TH CENTURY
(WOOD)
COMBINATION OF A WOODEN ARCH WITH A
MULTIPLE KING POST. (ARCH ALSO COM-
BINED WITH LATER WOODEN TRUSSES).
LENGTH: 50-175 FEET
15-50 METERS

TRUSS LEG BEDSTEAD

LATE 19TH-EARLY 20TH CENTURY
A PRATT WITH VERTICAL END POSTS IMBEDD-
ED IN THEIR FOUNDATIONS.

LENGTH: 30-100 FEET
9-30 METERS

LENTICULAR (PARABOLIC)

1878- EARLY 20TH CENTURY
A PRATT WITH BOTH TOP AND BOTTOM CHORDS
PARABOLICLY CURVED OVER THEIR ENTIRE
LENGTH.
LENGTH: 50-360 FEET
5-110 METERS

DOUBLE INTERSECTION WARREN

(LATTICE)
MID 19TH-20TH CENTURY
STRUCTURE IS INDETERMINATE. MEMBERS ACT
IN BOTH COMPRESSION AND TENSION. TWO
TRIANGULAR WEB SYSTEMS ARE SUPER IM-
POSED UPON EACH OTHER WITH OR WITHOUT VERTICALS
LENGTH: 75-400 FEET
23-120 METERS

TOWN LATTICE

1820- LATE 19TH CENTURY
(WOOD)
A SYSTEM OF WOODEN DIAGONALS WITH
NO VERTICALS. MEMBERS TAKE BOTH
COMPRESSION AND TENSION.
LENGTH: 50-220 FEET
15-66 METERS

PARKER

MID-LATE 19TH- 20TH CENTURY
A PRATT WITH A POLYGONAL TOP CHORD

LENGTH: 40-350 FEET
12-75 METERS

GREINER

1894- EARLY 20TH CENTURY
PRATT TRUSS WITH THE DIAGONALS RE-
PLACED BY AN INVERTED BOWSTRING TRUSS

LENGTH: 75-250 FEET
23-75 METERS

PEGRAM

1887 - EARLY 20TH CENTURY
A HYBRID BETWEEN THE WARREN AND PARKER
TRUSSES, UPPER CHORDS ARE ALL OF EQUAL
LENGTH.
LENGTH: 50-250 FEET
45-195 METERS

HOWE

1840- 20TH CENTURY
(WOOD, VERTICALS OF METAL)
DIAGONALS IN COMPRESSION, VERTICALS IN
TENSION.
LENGTH: 30-150 FEET
9-45 METERS

CAMELBACK

LATE 19TH-20TH CENTURY
A PARKER WITH A POLYGONAL TOP CHORD OF
EXACTLY FIVE SLOPES.

LENGTH: 100-500 FEET
30-90 METERS

DOUBLE INTERSECTION PRATT

1865- LATE 19TH CENTURY
(WHIPPLE, WHIPPLE-MURPHY, LINVILLE)
AN INCLINED END POST PRATT WITH DIAGONALS
THAT EXTEND ACROSS TWO PANELS.
LENGTH: 70-300 FEET
21-90 METERS

POST

1865- LATE 19TH CENTURY
A HYBRID BETWEEN THE WARREN AND THE
DOUBLE INTERSECTION PRATT

LENGTH: 100-300 FEET
30-90 METERS

BOWSTRING ARCH-TRUSS

1840- LATE 19TH CENTURY
A TIED ARCH WITH THE DIAGONALS SERVING
AS BRACING AND THE VERTICALS SUPPORT-
ING THE DECK.
LENGTH: 50-130 FEET
15-40 METERS

CAMELBACK

WITH SUBDIVIDED PANELS
LATE 19TH-EARLY 20TH CENTURY
A. A PENNSYLVANIA TRUSS WITH A POLY-
GONAL TOP CHORD OF EXACTLY FIVE SLOPES
B. SAME AS A. WITH INCLINED STRUTS.
LENGTH: 100-500 FEET
30-150 METERS

SCHWEDLER

LATE 19TH CENTURY
A DOUBLE INTERSECTION PRATT POSITION-
ED IN THE CENTER OF A PARKER.

LENGTH: 100-300 FEET
30-90 METERS

BOLLMAN

1852- MID-LATE 19TH CENTURY
(RARE)
VERTICALS IN COMPRESSION, DIAGONALS
IN TENSION. DIAGONALS RUN FROM END
POSTS TO EVERY POINT.
LENGTH: 75-100 FEET
23-30 METERS

WADDELL "A" TRUSS

LATE 19TH-EARLY 20TH CENTURY
EXPANDED VERSION OF THE KING POST
TRUSS. USUALLY MADE OF METAL

LENGTH: 25-75 FEET
8-23 METERS

KELLOGG

LATE 19TH CENTURY
A VARIATION OF THE PRATT WITH ADDITIONAL
DIAGONALS RUNNING FROM UPPER CHORD PAN-
EL POINTS TO THE CENTER OF THE LOWER
CHORDS.
LENGTH: 75-150 FEET
23-30 METERS

K-TRUSS

EARLY 20TH CENTURY
SO CALLED BECAUSE OF THE DISTINCTIVE OUT-
LINE OF THE STRUCTURAL MEMBERS.

LENGTH: 200-800 FEET
60-240 METERS

FINK

1851- MID - LATE 19TH CENTURY
(RARE)
VERTICALS IN COMPRESSION, DIAGONALS IN
TENSION, LONGEST DIAGONALS RUN FROM END
POSTS TO CENTER POINTS.
LENGTH: 75-100 FEET
23-45 METERS

WICHERT

1930- MID-LATE 20TH CENTURY
IDENTIFIED BY A CHARACTERISTIC PIN-
CONNECTED SUPPORT SYSTEM OVER THE
PIERS. TRUSS IS CONTINUOUS OVER PIERS.
LENGTH: 400-1000 FEET
122-305 METERS

TRUSSES
A STUDY BY THE
HISTORIC AMERICAN ENGINEERING RECORD

STEARNS

1890- EARLY 20TH CENTURY
SIMPLIFICATION OF THE TRUSS WITH VERTICALS
OMITTED AT ALTERNATE PANEL POINTS.

LENGTH: 50-200 FEET
15-60 METERS

bowstring truss, for example, was named after its arched bowlike appearance. The Baltimore truss was so called because it was used almost exclusively on the Baltimore–Ohio railroad line. The Thacher truss, designed in 1883, received its name from its inventor, Edwin Thacher.

Kings, Queens, and Waddell A Trusses

The most simple trusses were based on a triangle design. Requiring little material and easy to build, these rudimentary devices were effective in small towns or on remote roads but shared one fundamental flaw: they could support only very short spans. The King Post truss, using a dominant single vertical post in the center of the triangle, first appeared in the Middle Ages. It took several centuries for its second-generation counterpart, the Queen Post, to make it into documented history. The Queen Post was supported by two vertical posts on the deck. A little more sophisticated triangle variation called the Waddell A, named after J. A. L. Waddell, first appears in recorded history in the late nineteenth century. It added substruts and verticals to the basic King Post design.

The Pratt Truss

The Pratt truss was patented in 1844 by Caleb and Thomas Pratt, a father-and-son engineering team from Boston. This common truss is distinguished by most of its vertical members acting in compression and its diagonals, which leaned up and away from the center of the bridge, acting in tension. Many other trusses are based on this common Pratt design.

The Parker truss was a variation of the Pratt and was identical except for its polygonal upper profile. This arched modification reduced the amount of metal needed for the bridge yet made the bridge stronger. This more material-efficient design did not make the Pratt obsolete, because the Pratt, relying on uniform parts, was easier to put together and consequently less expensive to build.

The camelback truss and the Parker truss are often mistaken for each other, because, from a distance, their profiles looks pretty much the same.

Upon closer examination, one can see that the number of individual top chord pieces in the camelback has been reduced (usually to five) so that each top chord piece spans two panels of the truss. This minor change improved the standardization of the truss's parts without diminishing its strength.

Baltimore and Pennsylvania trusses were common on Midwest railroad lines. (The Baltimore–Ohio line and the Pennsylvania line, hence the names.) By adding substruts and ties to the Pratt design, both trusses were able to carry heavier loads, such as locomotives, over longer spans. The Baltimore is a subdivided modification of the basic Pratt design, and the Pennsylvania is a subdivided modification of the camelback.

One final Pratt variation is worthy of mention, not because of its unique design but more because of its unusual name. It is the Squire Whipple truss. Also known as a Whipple-Murphy or a Linville, and today more often called a double-intersection Pratt, the Squire Whipple extended its diagonals over two panels, increasing the overall efficiency of the truss and allowing it to accommodate longer spans. The double hatching, or crisscrossing effect, over the vertical posts of a Pratt is a dead giveaway for a Squire Whipple.

The Warren Truss

Patented in 1848 by two young Englishmen, James Warren and Willoughby Monzani, the Warren truss is simply an elegant series of isosceles triangles connected back-to-back, presenting a perfect profile of V's or W's, depending on how you look at it. Because the diagonals are leaning both toward and away from the center of the bridge, they are alternately in compression and tension. More often than not, secondary members bisect triangles to give the truss more strength.

In the same way that the Pratt truss was strengthened by extending diagonals over two or more panels, so, too, the Warren evolved creating the double- and sometimes triple-intersection Warren truss. When more and more diagonals were added, the truss began to look like latticework and was often called a lattice truss.

Metal Bridges That Seem to Defy Categorization

The bowstring arch truss, also developed by Squire Whipple, suspended the deck of the bridge with eyebars from an arched top chord, in effect creating a type of metal arch bridge.

The Howe truss reversed the angle of inclination of its diagonals from the classic Pratt design. Instead of leaning away from the center of the bridge, they leaned toward the center and consequently were in compression while the verticals were in tension.

The lenticular truss was a striking design by any standard. Its arched top chord and its lower mirror-image chord formed a lenslike parabola truss. Acting like suspension strands of a bowstring arch, its verticals extended from the top of the truss through its reverse arch to the deck of the bridge.

It doesn't take much imagination to understand where the K-truss got its name.

Some trusses are like optical illusions. Look carefully at the Stearns truss. Do you see a Warren design? Now, blink your eyes and look again. Does a Pratt appear? The Thacher can also trick our senses with similar double vision.

Such rare and exotic designs as the bowstring arch, the lenticular, the Stearns, the Thacher, and numerous others prove that bridge design was limited not so much by an engineer's imagination but more so by a community's pocketbook and the slow standardization of truss design that befell, as with all other public construction disciplines, the common metal-truss bridge.

Laws and the Organizations Overseeing Them

ISTEA

The Intermodal Surface Transportation Efficiency Act of 1991, commonly referred to as ISTEA ("ice tea") significantly changed the way the federal highway administration (FHWA) did business with the states. It gave each state more authority and flexibility in allocating federal funds for local transportation use.

> ISTEA has been called revolutionary and unprecedented in its empowerment of state and local officials to solve their specific transportation problems, flexibility in the use of funds by state and local governments, environmental enhancement, and planning and management systems that will enable our intermodal network to work more efficiently.
>
> —Lawrence Dwyer, *Intermodalism and ISTEA: The Challenges and the Changes*, 1994

ISTEA and subsequent replacement bills TEA-21 and SAFETEA-LU are of particular interest to the preservationist because they require states to use a minimum of 10 percent of their federal transportation funds for enhancement activities, such as the planting of wildflowers along a transportation corridor, converting an abandoned railroad line into a bike trail, or restoring an old depot. The word *enhancement* can open many doors to those trying to rehabilitate old things, and this includes the preservation of historic metal-truss bridges. The federal enhancement program has become the number one funding source for historic bridge restoration projects in the United States. More money comes from this one program than from all other sources combined. So, on a cold winter day, when you are out walking your bridge and wondering, "How can we ever raise enough money to save this thing?" think TEA.

STURAA

President Reagan signed the Surface Transportation and Uniform Relocation Assistance Act into law in 1987. Its impact on the restoration of historic bridges is neatly summarized in Paul Daniel Marriott's book, *Saving Historic Roads:*

> STURAA . . . contains two special provisions for protecting historic bridges. First, prior to the approval of federal funding for the demolition of any historic bridge, STURRA requires the bridge be made available to a "state, local, or responsible private entity" that would agree to maintain the bridge. Second, STURAA obligates the Federal Highway Administration to reimburse or make available to the new owner the costs of preserving or rehabilitating a historic bridge that is no longer used for motor vehicle traffic, up to the estimated cost of bridge demolition.
>
> —Paul Daniel Marriott, *Saving Historic Roads: Design and Policy Guidelines*
> (New York : John Wiley, 1998), 44

In other words, if the rehabilitation of a bridge is a realistic option, federal demolition money may be redirected to save the bridge rather than tear it down. This is more than good news. It is law.

AASHTO

The American Association of State Highway and Transportation Officials is

a nonprofit, nonpartisan association representing highway and transportation departments in the 50 states, the District of Columbia and Puerto Rico.
It represents all five transportation modes: air, highways, public transportation, rail and water. Its primary goal is to foster the development, operation
and maintenance of an integrated national transportation system.

—Bradly L. Mallory, AASHTO president, 2002

AASHTO (*"ash-tow"*) is to the transportation world what *Consumer
Reports* is to the common household. It takes a hard look at transportation
"product safety" and recommends solutions based on extensive testing of
construction materials and methods. It has no legal authority to impose
its findings on anyone. Each state must set its own standards. AASHTO is
merely an advisory organization. However, its long-standing reputability
among state and federal transportation officials has made it the gold standard
for transportation safety throughout the United States. If a preservationist
deviates from AASHTO, liability concerns may increase and professionals
might think twice about working on a non-standard project.

AASHTO is best known for its publication commonly called the Green
Book, more properly titled *A Policy on Geometric Design of Highways and
Streets.* Updated every few years, the Green Book recommends construction standards for everything from reflective coatings on road signs to metal
gauge minimums for overpass side rails. Transportation engineers rarely do
anything without first opening the Green Book. The Green Book does allow
a certain amount of flexibility, however, make sure you are working with
someone experienced in applying that flexibility. Most states also allow
design exceptions, which take into account that not every bridge came out
of the same cookie cutter. Design exceptions allow an engineer to safely
address a non-standard item.

NCHRP

The National Cooperative Highway Research Program is an investigative and research organization dedicated to solving transportation problems. It is voluntarily funded by state transportation departments and is made up of top experts in each of its fields of study. The NCHRP collaborates with state transportation departments, the AASHTO Standing Committee on Research (SCOR), and various federal highway administrators in selecting and executing its research projects.

NCHRP is significant to bridge preservation because it is a working organization that regularly tackles, in a disciplined and academic way, all types of problems associated with land transportation, including the care of old bridges. Unlike small communities or even regional authorities with limited resources, the NCHRP is large enough to undertake thorough studies into bridge construction and rehabilitation problems and regularly publishes the results of these studies for the entire transportation community.

NHPA

The National Historic Preservation Act was passed by Congress on October 15, 1966, and declared:

> the historical and cultural foundations of the Nation should be preserved as a living part of our community life and development in order to give a sense of orientation to the American people. . . . The preservation of this irreplaceable heritage is in the public interest so that its vital legacy of cultural, educational, aesthetic, inspirational, economic, and energy benefits will be maintained and enriched for future generations of Americans.
>
> —NHPA16 U.S.C. 470 Section 1

Under the auspices of the Department of the Interior, the NHPA mandates that each state implement a statewide historic preservation program to be administered by a governor-appointed state historic preservation officer, SHPO, and overseen by a state review board.

This act also empowers the secretary of the interior to maintain a National Register of Historic Places, which affords special, albeit nonlegal, protection to properties deemed National Historic Landmarks. Although this law does not make owners preserve historic bridges, it requires them to study alternatives to demolition when federal funds kick in for any work. Your state also keeps a list of registered landmarks and may even have a state inventory list of historic bridges. If your bridge is registered as a national or state historic landmark or if you believe it may qualify for such recognition, political, legal, and financial support for your project may be greatly increased.

HAER

As part of the National Park Service, the Historic American Engineering Record (HAER) is charged with creating and collecting records on engineering sites in America. The HAER collection is housed in the Library of Congress and includes measured drawings, photographs, and written histories of engineering artifacts, some of which are truss bridges.

Portland, Michigan's Enhancement Application

Describe the Existing Transportation Facility and the Proposed Work

Existing:

The proposed path is along an abandoned railroad corridor, which the City has acquired. The railroad crossed the Looking Glass River east of the Divine Highway bridge on an acute angle. The bridge at this location consisted of several timber spans, over 260 feet in total length. The bridge and the timber bents were removed by the Railroad a few years ago.

The railroad crossed the Grand River on the two span steel bridge which is still in place. The total length of this bridge is 340 feet. The rails have been removed but the ties are still in place.

Proposed:

To provide for the pedestrian/bike trail, it is proposed to cross the Looking Glass River at a location where the bridge would be perpendicular to the river so that the bridge is shorter and has less impact on the flow of the river. The proposed location starts near the location of the north abutment of the removed bridge and crosses the river to the top of the bank on the south side. The river cross section at this location is approximately 110 feet from the top of the bank to the edge of the railroad embankment. After crossing the river the path would then turn and run along the top of the south bank approximately 200 feet until it re-connects with the abandoned railroad grade.

To provide the bridge for the Looking Glass River crossing, it is proposed to restore the Burroughs Road Bridge, to be provided by the Kent County Road Commission. The Burroughs Road Bridge is currently located over the Flat River, 3 miles north of Lowell, Michigan. The structure is a two span, pony truss bridge, 121 feet long from abutment to abutment. The bridge was built in 1905 by the Groton Bridge and Manufacturing Company who also built the Bridge Street Bridge in Portland. The bridge is now closed to vehicles due to the very poor condition of the concrete abutments. In 1991 the Kent County Road Commission applied for and was selected to receive Critical Bridge funds to replace the Burroughs Road bridge. Subsequent to the selection, investigation by the Michigan Bureau of History indicated that the bridge was eligible for inclusion on the National Register of Historic Places.

The Road Commission has studied the following alternatives:

1. Rehabilitation of the bridge in place for roadway use.
2. Realigning the roadway and leaving the bridge in place for pedestrian/fishing uses.
3. Relocating the bridge to another location.
4. Demolishing the bridge.

Alternative 1 cannot provide the County with the necessary bridge loading and widths to satisfy FHWA criteria for Critical Bridge funds.

Alternative 2 would require a longer bridge due to the widening of the Flat River downstream of the bridge. Also due to the natural river designation of the Flat River the DNR would like a replacement bridge to clear span the river. The revised alignment would require a very long and expensive bridge to clear the river.

The road commission does not have any suitable locations at this time for relocating the bridge in Kent County to satisfy *alternative 3*, but they are willing to allow Portland to use the bridge if the County decides not to restore it.

Alternative 4 is a last resort in case none of the three other alternatives can be worked out.

The Road Commission is meeting October 19th to decide which of the above alternatives it wishes to pursue. They have provided a conditional agreement to provide the bridge to Portland if they do not wish to restore it in place.

Restoration of the Burroughs Road bridge for the Looking Glass river crossing in Portland would provide an excellent alternative to demolition of the bridge and would serve the path project very well. The length allows the bridge to be built above the 100 year flood level of the river. The clear width of 13 feet 6 inches is excellent for the path. The timber deck would either be salvaged or replaced with new timber and a pedestrian railing would be added to the bridge. After steel repairs and painting are completed the restored bridge would be capable of supporting pedestrian and maintenance vehicle loading. Furthermore, by providing a restored historic bridge the pathway will be connected to three different restored truss bridges, thus providing a unique theme to the path.

The existing Railroad Bridge over the Grand River is owned by the city and would be converted to carry the pedestrian/bike trail traffic. The proposed work will include removal of the railroad ties, painting the steel floor girders and the steel truss, placing a 12 feet wide reinforced concrete deck on a galvanized steel deck, and installing pedestrian/bike railing on both sides of the deck. Lighting will be provided on the bridge. Substructures will be inspected and repaired if necessary. This bridge was constructed prior to 1915.

The Bridge Street Bridge was rehabilitated in 1990. Historical research and documentation for the bridge was prepared and submitted to the National Park Service, Historic American Engineering Record (HAER) prior to the restoration. Based on this research an ASCE Historic Civil Engineering Landmark was awarded to the City. It is proposed to construct a post for installing the historic landmark plaque on the northwest wing-wall of the bridge. It is also proposed to acquire a Michigan Historical Marker, with a narrative of the history of the bridge and have it installed.

It is also proposed to route part of the river trail path under the west end of the Bridge Street and Grand River Avenue Bridges. The Bridge Street path would be constructed using pre-cast concrete or timber panels, supported by the steel sheet piling in front of the west abutment and anchored into the abutment. To provide for an 8 foot wide path the planks would cantilever out from the sheet pile approximately 4 feet over the edge of the river. Railings would be installed and would be removable for the winter months. The grade separation for Grand River Avenue would be concrete placed on rip-rap. The path would be 8 feet wide and would have removable railings. Once beyond the bridge, the trail would be placed on piles to minimize impact on the river bottom.

Complete an Environmental Review

REVIEW OF ENVIRONMENTAL FACTORS:	NO	YES
1. Displacement of residence or business	✔	
2. Disruption of neighbors	✔	
3. Agriculture	✔	
4. Recreational lands	✔	
5. Historic and Archaeological	✔	
6. Wetlands	✔	
7. Streams/Lakes/Drains	✔	
8. Floodplains	✔	
9. Environmental Permits Required	✔	
10. Coastal zone	✔	
11. Endangered species	✔	
12. Tree removal	✔	
13. Inconsistent with local development plans	✔	
14. Change in developed land uses	✔	
15. Change in access control or level	✔	
16. Change in facilities for pedestrians or bicyclists	✔	
17. Detour/temporary road/ramp closure	✔	
18. Hazardous waste	✔	
19. Noise	✔	
20. Air quality	✔	
21. Subject of controversy	✔	
22. Any other issue	✔	

Impact Evaluation: Due to the construction the project will require DNR permits for wetlands, streams and floodplain impacts. A preliminary site review was conducted with the City and DNR, Land and Water Management Division representatives on April 15, 1992. Based on the review the following recommendations were made to minimize impacts of the project;

1. The pathway in the floodplain will be constructed with minimal filling. Details of parking areas and canoe launch site will be reviewed with the DNR at a later time.
2. The grade separation under Grand River Avenue will be constructed using heavy riprap with a path width of 10 feet. The path under the bridge will have steep side slopes to minimize filling.
3. The path north of the Grand River Avenue bridge, running along the edge of the Grand River, shall be constructed on piles to avoid filling of river bottomland.
4. The bridge crossing the Looking Glass River should cross perpendicular (or very small skew) to the river flow. A single span would be preferred but a pier would be allowed if necessary, depending on span lengths.

Explain the Benefits of Proposed Project

The plan is part of the City Master Plan with the objective of providing pedestrian and bicycle access throughout the community. The project connects the downtown area with the high school and the major city recreational facilities. In addition to being a recreation facility, the project is anticipated to be used extensively by residents as a means of transportation to the City parks and schools.

The lighting and grade separation will provide a much safer environment and extend the hours of use each day. The City has the support of business leaders, through the DDA, as well as support from the residents.

Prepared by HH Engineering, Al Halbeisen, Consultant-Engineer

Study of Historic Bridges to Be Renovated and Relocated for Use on the Portland Trail System over the Grand River in the City of Portland, Michigan

Purpose

The purpose of this study is to evaluate the feasibility and cost of relocating one of the following bridges, either Kent Street, Turner Road or Goodwin Road, to a site along the I-96 corridor over the Grand River. The bridge would be used as a non-motorized trail bridge for the City of Portland Trail System. All three of the bridges are located in Ionia County over the Grand River and are under the jurisdiction of the Ionia County Road Commission. Only the Kent Street Bridge is currently open to traffic. All three bridges are on the Michigan Historic Bridge inventory list. Preliminary estimates for the City of Portland share of the construction costs for removing, relocating and restoring each bridge for use at the proposed site are included in the appendix [not provided here]. The estimates consider the differences in funding available for each bridge and the differences in bridge lengths and structural conditions. Due to the size of each bridge it is assumed that they would need to be disassembled before relocating.

Proposed Site of Portland Trail System over Grand River, Section 32, Portland Township

The proposed location of the bridge would be just inside the north I-96 right-of-way line. The I-96 bridge at this location is a four span steel girder structure that spans over the Grand River and over Market Street. The total length of the bridge is 414 feet, with an 81.5-foot span over Market, and 101-, 130-, and 101.5-foot spans over the Grand River floodplain. The river is approximately 190 feet wide from bank to bank. There are two piers in the Grand River.

The proposed City of Portland Trail will be along Market Street, which is at elevation 725 feet under the I-96 bridge. I-96 roadway is at approximately elevation 750 feet. It would be desirable to span over the floodplain and either match the location of piers with the existing bridge or keep piers out of the main channel flow so that hydraulic impacts would be minimal. There are residences immediately upstream of I-96. The approximate high water is elevation 717 feet.

The floodplain width at this location is approximately 280 feet. The Goodwin Road Bridge is about 20 feet longer, but would require constructing a pier in the Grand River and the pier would not align with the two existing piers in the river. Using either the Kent Street or Turner Road bridges would require additional approach spans to go over the floodplain, however both of these bridges could span the main channel. For the comparison of alternatives we will assume that the total length of main and approach spans will need to be 300 feet for all three alternatives.

Kent Street over Grand River, Section 4, Danby Township, South of Portland

The Kent Street Bridge is a Parker Through Truss, built in 1907. Information on truss types and terminology is included in the appendix of

Table 5. Kent Street over Grand River, Engineer's Estimate of Probable Cost

General	QUANTITY	UNIT COST	TOTAL COST
Mobilization, existing bridge site	1 lsum	$5,000.00	$5,000.00
Remove deck and stringers	1 lsum	$10,000.00	$10,000.00
Remove truss from foundation	1 lsum	$37,000.00	$37,000.00
Disassemble and transport	1 lsum	$15,000.00	$15,000.00
SUBTOTAL			$67,000.00
Substructure			
Backfill, structure, CIP	70 cyd	$15.00	$1,050.00
Excavation, foundation	80 cyd	$12.50	$1,000.00
Timber bent, approach span pier	2 each	$5.000.00	$10,000.00
Timber abutments and wingwalls	2 each	$15,000.00	$30,000.00
Pile, steel, furnished and driven, 12 in.	480 ft	$25.00	$12,000.00
Test pile, steel, 12 in.	4 each	$500.00	$2,000.00
Pile driving equipment, furnished	1 lsum	$5,000.00	$5,000.00
Substructure concrete	100 cyd	$400.00	$40,000.00
Riprap, plain	150 syd	$50.00	$7,500.00
SUBTOTAL			$108,550.00
Superstructure			
Structural steel, mixed, furnish and fabricate	7500 lbs	$4.00	$30,000.00
Structural steel, furnish and fabricate, pins	500 lbs	$5.00	$2,500.00
Structural steel, retrofit and erect	1 lsum	$65,000.00	$65,000.00
Timber deck, furnished and erected, 8 in.	2640 sft	$30.00	$79,200.00
Timber approach spans (12 feet wide w/railings)	80 lft	$600.00	$48,000.00
Railing, pedestrian	440 lft	$75.00	$33,000.00
Steel structure, cleaning, type 4	12650 sft	$6.00	$75,900.00
Steel structure, coating, type 4	12650 sft	$4.00	$50,600.00
Field repair of damaged coating	1 lsum	$1,000.00	$1,000.00
SUBTOTAL			$385,200.00
Miscellaneous			
Structural steel, furnish and fabricate, pins	500 lbs	$5.00	$2,500.00
Mobilization max.	1 lsum	$30,000.00	$30,000.00
Contingencies and other misc. items	1 lsum	$24,250.00	$24,250.00
SUBTOTAL			$54,250.00
TOTAL			**$615.000.00**

KEY: lsum = lump sum; cyd = cubic yard; ft = feet; syd = square yard; lbs = pounds; sft = square feet; lft = lineal feet this report. The term *Parker* refers to the use of a polygonal top chord on what is essentially a Pratt truss. The top chord gives the bridge an arched appearance. The builder, Wynkoop & McGormly of Toledo, Ohio, was a significant Midwestern metal truss bridge manufacturer during the last quarter of the nineteenth century into the early decades of the twentieth century. The Turner Road bridge, another Parker Through Truss, was built by the same firm.

The single-span bridge consists of 11 panels of 20 feet. With abutments the total length is 224 feet. The existing deck is timber and has a clear width of 15.7 feet. The bridge is posted for a weight limit of 3 tons. The bridge has had several repairs to truss members to keep it in service. Several verticals have been damaged by vehicle collisions and have either been repaired by replacement with new (and different) members or have been left in bent condition. The horizontal lateral bracing under the deck in several bays is either loose or has been replaced. The steel stringers and floor beams are heavily rusted and may have loss of structural section.

The cost of mobilizing equipment, removing the bridge from the foundations and disassembly would be eligible for Critical Bridge funds in conjunction with the Ionia County Road Commission project to build a new bridge at this site. Bidding for the project is anticipated by the fall of 2001, with construction in 2002. An Environmental Assessment has been completed, with provisions for using the bridge on Portland's Trail System or for removal and marketing of the bridge.

A structural analysis was performed for the existing truss members and it was determined that the original bridge members can carry the loading of 85 pounds per square foot required for pedestrian loading. Deteriorated or damaged members should be repaired or replaced as part of the restoration work.

Other work required to restore the bridge for pedestrian use would include testing and possible replacement of the connecting pins, cleaning and coating the steel truss and floor beams, replacement of the existing timber plank deck and steel stringers with a new timber deck panel system, addition of pedestrian railings, and construction of new substructures and approach spans. The approach spans would consist of timber deck panels similar to the panels on the main span. Three 20-foot spans would be needed on the west approach and one 20-foot span on the east approach. The new deck on the main bridge and approach spans would be 12 feet wide to minimize loading on the bridge and to decrease the cost of the project.

The total estimated cost for the project is $615,000 for the structure and the City of Portland share of the estimated construction cost is $293,790.

Turner Road over Grand River, Section 23, Danby Township, Southeast of Portland

Turner Road Bridge is a Parker Through Truss, built in 1910 and reconstructed in 1969. The single span bridge consists of 9 panels of 22 feet and 8 inches. With abutments the total length is 208 feet. The existing deck is cast-in-place concrete, and has a clear width of 16 feet.

The bridge has been closed for many years due to the poor condition of the concrete deck. The main truss members are in good condition and appear to be the original members. The stringers and floor beams are in fair condition (possibly replaced in 1969). There is some rusting and deterioration at the top flanges of the beams.

Access to the site is difficult. From the south the approach would be through farm fields and pastures and would require some clearing to access the bridge for removal. There is a relatively level area for setting the bridge down after removal for disassembly. From the north the approach is shorter, but is steep and does not have a good area for setting the bridge down after removal for disassembly. The cost of mobilizing equipment, removing the bridge from the foundations and disassembly would be part of the city's project. The cast-in-place concrete deck will need to be carefully removed prior to removing the bridge from the site. It would be possible to apply for additional MDOT Enhancement funds for the existing site access and removal work since this site work was not included in the original application, but the funds would be for fiscal year 2003.

The work required to restore the bridge for pedestrian use would include minor repair of damaged truss members and pins, cleaning and coating the steel truss and floor beams, replacement of the deck and stringers with a new timber deck panel system, addition of pedestrian railings, and construction of new substructures and approach spans. The approach spans would consist of timber deck panels similar to the panels on the main span. Three

20-foot spans would be needed on the west approach and two 18-foot spans on the east approach. The new deck on the main bridge and approach spans would be 12 feet wide to minimize loading on the bridge and to decrease the cost of the project.

The total estimated cost for the project is $555,000 for the structure and the City of Portland share of the estimated construction cost is about $294,150, assuming that the Enhancement funding could be applied for the removal work at the current grant rate of 53 percent.

Since the bridge is currently closed to traffic it is in no immediate danger of demolition. If further development of the City Trail System requires another bridge over the Looking Glass River then this would be a good bridge to consider for use. It could also be used as a backup for this project in the event that the Kent Street Bridge is damaged during removal to the extent that it could not be salvaged.

Goodwin Road over Grand River, Section 8 and 17, Portland Township, North of Portland

The Goodwin Road Bridge is a Pratt Through Truss, built in 1909. The bridge consists of two spans of 150 feet for a total length of 300 feet. Each span consists of 10 panels of 15 feet. The existing deck is timber and has a clear width of 13 feet.

The bridge has been closed for many years, possibly due to the very poor condition of the substructures. The timber deck is missing many boards. The steel truss members have very little paint and are rusted, but the rust is not concentrated at connection points to the extent that major replacement of members would be required. The steel stringers are rusted to the point that a new deck system or steel stringers would be necessary.

Access to the site is not difficult from either direction. There is a relatively level area for setting the bridge down after removal for disassembly. The river at this location is relatively deep and would allow the use of a barge to carry a crane to the center pier if necessary for removal of the truss. The cost of mobilizing equipment, removing the bridge from the foundations and disassembly would be part of the city's project. It would be possible to apply for additional MDOT Enhancement funds for the existing site access and removal work since this site work was not included in the original application, but the funds would be for fiscal year 2003.

The work required to restore the bridge for pedestrian use would include repair and/or replacement of damaged truss members and pins, cleaning and coating the steel truss and floor beams, replacement of the deck and stringers with a new timber deck panel system, addition of pedestrian railings, and construction of new substructures. The new deck would be 12 feet wide to minimize loading on the bridge and to decrease the cost of the project.

The total estimated cost for the project is $565,000 for the structure and the City of Portland share of the estimated construction cost is about $299,450, assuming that the Enhancement funding could be applied for the removal work at the current grant rate of 53 percent.

Since the bridge is currently closed to traffic it is in no immediate danger of demolition. If other pedestrian trail systems require a bridge then this would be a good bridge to consider for use.

Conclusions and Recommendations

Each of the three bridges has advantages and disadvantages such that the decision on the best alternative is not obvious. Differences in the funding available, site access, demolition costs, structural repairs, deck systems, maintenance and total bridge and span lengths are all factors which have had to be considered. Cost estimates based on these factors have been prepared, but the difference in cost to the City of Portland between any of the alternatives is minor. The final cost could vary depending on the contractors bidding the project.

The Kent Street Bridge has the longest span to clear the Grand River, although Turner Road Bridge is only 16 feet shorter. Both of these would require short approach spans to avoid filling in the floodplain. Goodwin Road Bridge would span the entire floodplain but would require a pier in the Grand River. This would make it more difficult to obtain permits from the Michigan Department of Environmental Quality (MDEQ), especially since the pier would not match the location of the I-96 bridge piers.

The Turner Road Bridge is in the best structural condition of the three, but it is has the most difficult site access and has a concrete deck that would be more difficult to remove. The Kent Street Bridge has significant deterioration, but the access for removal would be included in the Ionia County Road Commission project to build a new bridge. The Kent Street Bridge appears to have been designed for higher uniform loads, making it a more durable structure than the other bridges. The Goodwin Road Bridge, although closed to traffic, has relatively good access for removal. Deterioration of the trusses is moderate and there are no significant damaged members.

All three of the bridges would need a new deck system. We have evaluated options for the deck system and propose that a timber panel system be used that would replace the steel stringers and deck plank systems. Another option for the deck system is to use galvanized steel deck pans with a bituminous surface. This system requires the salvage and painting of the stringer beams. The advantage of the timber system is reduced dead load on the structure and elimination of the cost of repairing/replacing and painting the steel stringers. The cost comparison of the deck systems is close and the selection can be reviewed in more detail during the design phase of the project.

Beyond the historic designation, the aesthetic qualities of the three bridges vary. Both the Kent Street and Turner Road Bridges are Parker Through Trusses, which use a polygonal top chord. The varied height of the top chord gives the bridges an arched appearance. These two bridges are higher than the Goodwin Road Bridge and would therefore have more visibility from I-96. The Goodwin Road Bridge has a straight top chord and with its shorter span length has a shorter vertical height. Kent Street Bridge, due to its history of vehicle collision damage, has several replaced/repaired members that detract from its appearance. However, after disassembly, replacing these damaged members with structural members that match the originals would be feasible and is included in the cost estimate.

Primarily due to the State Historic Preservation Office (SHPO) and MDEQ regulatory issues and local preference, the Kent Street Bridge would be the best to be restored for use on the City of Portland Trail System. Although the total cost is higher, the City of Portland share of the cost is slightly lower due to the use of Critical Bridge funds to remove the bridge from it's current foundations and disassemble it. The Kent Street Bridge is a better fit for the site, has the support of the State Historic Preservation Office to be used for the project, and has more local support due its visibility and proximity to the city.

The Turner Road Bridge could be used as a backup for this project in the event that the Kent Street Bridge is damaged during removal to the extent that it could not be salvaged, or the bridge could be used for another location in the future.

The Goodwin Road Bridge does not fit this site well but could be a good bridge for another trail project.

To reduce the loads on the bridge we propose that the new deck be only 12 feet wide. Although Michigan's SHPO has opposed using a narrower deck on other projects we feel there are advantages that make this a worthwhile option to insist upon. In addition to reducing dead and live loads and reducing the cost of the deck, a narrower deck separates the new elements (deck and railing) from the historic truss structure and allows better views of the bridge parts (pin connections, floor beams and lower chords) that are often hidden by decks that extend the full width of the floor beams.

March 2001, HH Engineering Ltd.

Suggested Reading

General Interest

Black, Archibald. *The Story of Bridges.* New York, 1936.

Cooper, James L. *Iron Monuments to Distant Posterity—Indiana's Metal Bridges, 1870–1930.* Indianapolis: Indiana Historical Bureau, 1987.

Danko, George M. *Development of the Truss Bridge, 1820–1930, with a Focus toward Wisconsin.* Madison, Wisconsin: State Historic Preservation Office, State Historical Society of Wisconsin, 1976.

DeLony, Eric. *Landmark American Bridges.* New York: American Society of Civil Engineers, 1993.

Edwards, Llewellyn Nathaniel. *A Record of the History and Evolution of Early American Bridges.* Orono, Maine, 1959.

Hyde, Charles K. *Historic Highway Bridges of Michigan.* Detroit: Wayne State University Press, 1993.

Marriot, Paul Daniel. *Saving Historic Roads: Design and Policy Guidelines.* New York: John Wiley, 1998.

Plowden, David. *Bridges: The Spans of North America.* New York, 1974.

Steinman, David B., and Sara Ruth Watson. *Bridges and Their Builders.* New York, 1957.

Weitzman, David. *Traces of the Past—A Field Guide to Industrial Archaeology.* New York, 1980.

Truss Bridge Construction and Engineering

Bigelow, Lawrence N. "Fifty-Year Development—Construction of Steel Truss Bridges." *Journal of the Construction Division* 101 (June 1975): 239–58.
Boller, Alfred Pancoast. *Practical Treatise on the Construction of Iron Highway Bridges, for the Use of Town Committees.* New York, 1876.
Ketchum, Milo Smith. *The Design of Highway Bridges and the Calculation of Stress in Bridge Trusses.* New York, 1909.
Steinman, David B. *Fifty Years of Progress in Bridge Engineering.* New York, 1929.
Tyrrell, Henry Grattan. *History of Bridge Engineering.* Chicago, 1911.
Waddell, J. A. L. *The Designing of Ordinary Highway Bridges.* New York, 1884.

Metal-Truss Bridge Restoration

Chamberlin, William P. *Historic Highway Bridge Preservation Practices.* Washington, D.C.: National Academy Press, 1999.
Cooper, J. L., ed. *Restoring Historic Metal Truss Bridges: A Handbook for Keeping Faith with Their Makers.* Indianapolis: Indiana Division of Historic Preservation and Archaeology, 2001.
Hatfield, F. J. "Engineering for Rehabilitation of Historic Metal Truss Bridges." *Welding Innovation* 18, no. 3 (2001): 10–15.
Holt, Joseph. "Flame Straightening: A Friend in Need." *Welding Engineer* 40, no. 10 (October, 1955).
Jefferson, T. B.. *Metals and How to Weld Them*, 2nd ed. Cleveland: James F. Lincoln Arc Welding Foundation, 1990.
Melick, C. A. "Old Steel Road Bridges Restored by Welding." *Engineering News-Record* 106 (June 1, 1933): 706–8.
The Procedure Handbook of Arc Welding, Design and Practice. Cleveland: Lincoln Electric Company, 1933.

Simmons, David A. "'The Continuous Clatter': Practical Field Riveting." *IA: The Journal of the Society for Industrial Archeology* 23, no. 2 (1997).

Weibe, Melvin. "The Rivet Gang." *The Anvil's Ring* (Fall 1994).

Index